Eamon O'Donnell has been a management consultant for over thirty years. Through his work in staff and customer relations and in the management of organisational change he has found that a good story is more powerful than complex theories and dull statistical analysis.

He holds a BA degree and HDip in Education from UCD, and an MA degree in Organisation Behaviour from Trinity College Dublin.

In 1985, he established RMS Consulting to advise clients in the public, private and not-for-profit sectors. Clients include ESB, Aer Lingus, Irish Life, Nestlé (Ireland) Ltd, Industrial Computing Machines (ICM), and the Special Olympics.

He has lectured in the Irish Management Institute for over twenty years during which time he has developed a series of customised management development programmes for senior personnel in the European Commission.

In 1993, he was contracted by the European Commission to facilitate the development of the Commission's strategic approach to the allocation of £2 billion structural funds to Ireland. He was also contracted by the European Foundation for the Improvement of Living and Working Conditions as rapporteur to an expert group on the changing roles and functions of middle management.

A keen sportsman, he gained his colours for UCD in athletics and in the early 1980s organised some of the first racehorse syndicates in Ireland under his company Racing Management Services. He has had winners at most of the leading Irish racecourses.

To Sinbad & Seamus,

From The Brother of a Famous Author

Wishing you a Season of
Contented Goodwill for
Christmas 2012
The Main Thing is To Keep
The Main Thing, the Main Thing

Hugh O'Carroll

Dedicated to Mary

STOP
howling at the moon

Eamon O'Donnell

Cartoons by Terry Willers

ONSTREAM PUBLICATIONS
Currabaha, Cloghroe, Co. Cork, Ireland
www.onstream.ie

Text and cartoons © Eamon O'Donnell, 2007

1 89768 567 X

978 1 89768 567 9

2 4 6 8 10 9 7 5 3 1

Printed in England by CPD

Contents

First Thought

Man stand around for long time
with mouth open waiting for
roast duck to fly in.

(Ancient Chinese Proverb)

Dedication

To my wife, Mary, for her patience, understanding and good humour before, during and after the writing of this book.

Acknowledgements

To all my friends, from whom I have learned that there is only one way to make a long story short – a lesson I have happily ignored while still trusting our friendship remains intact.

Introduction

Stop Howling at the Moon is a book of ordinary, every-day stories that have influenced my life; stories I have collected and subsequently told and retold to help the listener gain insights into the possibilities of life; stories that will help make these possibilities a reality for those who are parenting, managing, teaching, coaching or consulting others as individuals or in organisations.

Organisations, be they family, voluntary, social or business, have one thing in common: the desire of the members to live in harmony and to collaborate to achieve the organisation's goals. Ask those in charge what is the most stressful aspect of their life and many will say it is rearing children or managing people and the apparently inevitable confrontation that comes with that responsibility. What many people fail to realise is that in every one-to-one relationship they may be fifty percent of the problem, but also more than fifty percent of the solution.

Where conflict arises it is easier to blame others than change your behaviour but it is easier to change your behaviour than to change someone else's. Blame has no part to play in developing harmonious relationships and a non-confrontational environment. These stories will allow people to distance themselves from the blame game, to understand the complexities of relationships, view frequently recurring problems through a fresh lens and build an environment which encourages creative problem solving. The stories are for those who are prepared to explore the mystery of life, to imagine and to move forward rather than recall endlessly why that is not possible. In that sense this book is future focused and is for visionaries, not historians.

When things are not functioning well in your life or your organisation, and every corrective action that can be taken has been taken yet the problem still remains, what is the problem? In all probability it is that the decision makers are locked into a fixed way of thinking; a way of thinking – First Order Thinking – which is rational, which exclusively focuses on analysis and logic, and where the required actions to bring about change are obvious and self-evident. This approach leads to solutions that usually demand working harder and faster and doing things better, not differently. It is an exercise of the mind. The mind loves explanations and order. First Order Thinking is a problem-solving approach which is necessary but not sufficient when addressing the complexities of life, living and organisational dynamics.

Second Order Thinking comes into play where the self-evident solutions fail. It goes beyond the rational and attempts to bring about a changed consciousness and new awareness. Einstein said, 'no problem can be solved from the same consciousness that created it, therefore you have to change people's consciousness of the problem.' Second Order Thinking often runs counter to all logic and is grounded in insight. It is frequently experienced through intuition or a leap of faith. Intuition and insight follow reflection and an acknowledgement and acceptance of our experience gained through life.

The stories and anecdotes in this book encapsulate my life experiences, reflections and some of the insights I have gained from them. I have commented on each story, sharing why I found it magical, memorable and invaluable to me personally and as a manager and consultant. Toscanini, one of the great conductors, said, 'It is more important to have the score in your head than your head in the score.' So to help retention and recall I have tried to capture the essence under the trigger phrase 'Get This'.

The book is designed to be read in no particular sequence – it is, after all, about mystery, magic and the development of Second Order Thinking. Dip into it and browse through it at your leisure. Read what grabs your attention and I suggest you then reflect on a story and consider what's going on in your life, your home, your workplace, and your environment, from a different consciousness. Listen to your own advice and decide what action you think is appropriate. Einstein, on being reminded that he had set the same examination questions for the same students two years running, commented, 'The questions may be the same but the answers have changed.' Each time you reflect on one of

Introduction

these stories you may see things differently; it may be that your life has moved on. We need to allow ourselves to move on, to give ourselves permission to visualise, to dream, to go to the frontiers of our imagination and take courageous action.

In the hurdy gurdy of everyday life we don't allow sufficient space to imagine. Many organisations are on the merger trail, the acquisition trail, the upsizing trail, the downsizing trail, the vertical or horizontal integration trail or the rationalisation trail. As long as you are on some trail or other you have lots of momentum, lots of hustle and bustle, with little or no time to imagine. In fact you are not required to imagine or be inspired but only to replicate. Others may easily fall into a rut because of the humdrum of their everyday lives and never lift their heads to see where they are going. It is only when we stop we think! These stories are there to entertain you, to stop you, to stimulate your imagination and to engage your soul. The soul loves stories and playfulness.

You can engage your soul and re-imagine while wheeling the buggy, the supermarket or golf trolley, on the train, on the plane, in the bath, the shower or the bed. These stories require reflection, will stretch your imagination, present options and encourage different choices. There is great safety in a good story and many unspeakable issues have been revealed and resolved in a safe way through a timely story. Storytelling in the musical, oral or written tradition is a cornerstone of many cultures. I believe storytelling plays a subtle and unique role in Irish life and is central to the development of both personal values and management culture. It also, as can be seen, allows complex issues to be addressed safely and with sensitivity.

Chapter 1

Go Put the Kettle on

1 _It Never Rains But it Pours_

Michael, a reputable thinker, a successful business-man and a perfectionist by nature, was desperately unhappy. He sought a meeting with Brother Anthony the Guru who was noted for his wisdom and was living a humble life in the seclusion of the monastery, high on the mountaintop. On meeting Brother Anthony, Michael blurted out his plight: he had everything he could ever want from life but still was not content. He urgently wanted to become enlightened! Brother Anthony calmly advised him to waste no time, go out immediately into the courtyard, tilt his head back, raise both his hands to Heaven and repeatedly ask God for enlightenment.

Later, when he passed through the courtyard, Brother Anthony saw that his most recent disciple was some-what agitated. 'How are you getting on?' he enquired.

'Dreadful,' replied Michael. 'I have been out here for over an hour, my hands raised to the heavens, I am feeling stiff, sore and I am hoarse. The rain is running down my arms and into my chest, my clothes are destroyed, I am miserable and I am not one bit enlightened. In fact, if you really want to know, right now I'm standing here feeling a proper fool!'

'Well,' reflected Brother Anthony. 'You know Michael, for the first day that's not bad.'

1 *It Never Rains But it Pours*

SO YOU THINK YOU'VE GOT IT ...

Sometimes in life people just don't get it. It is the guru's role to comfort the demented and dement the comfortable. Resistance can be manifested in many ways and is often masqueraded in confusion. What is clear to everyone else is not always clear to us. If we do get a revelation, a flash of inspiration, enlightenment or experience a breakthrough, we can often be left feeling a bit foolish and somewhat vulnerable. To move forward we should focus on the breakthrough and not the foolishness.

> GET THIS:
> LEARNING CAN BE FUN BUT MOST OF
> THE TIME IT IS HELL

2 *You Got Your Man*

In an interview for a management position in a new company, Jack was asked by the chief executive, 'what would you do if one of your supervisors came to work in a drunken condition?'

Jack quickly replied, 'I would take him aside, give him several cups of coffee, call a taxi and discretely send him home. When he returned to work the next day I would call him in, explain the position to him and give him a verbal warning …'

'Very good,' said the chief executive.

Jack continued quickly, 'If it happened again I would …'

'It's ok,' said the chief executive, 'I am suitably impressed. I have a flight to Amsterdam in an hour or so. You will hear from us by the end of the week.'

The company offered Jack the job and he duly accepted.

A week later as the chief executive was walking down Grafton Street he spotted Jack, congratulated him and said how he was looking forward to working with him.

'By the way,' he said, 'I was impressed with your reply on the handling of the drunk. Sorry I had to stop you short, what was the finish to your answer?'

'I would call him in, give him a written warning and if it happened again I would then dismiss him,' said Jack.

'Excellent,' said the chief executive, 'where did you learn all that?'

2 *You Got Your Man*

'Nowhere,' said Jack, 'that's what they did with me in my last job.'

The urgent demands may cause a sleepless night but if not given the proper time and attention the important ones will cause you sleepless months. Nothing is more important than the hiring of good staff and it ought to be a rigorous process and given your full attention. Don't take your eye off the ball and get distracted by a round of golf or a jolly to Amsterdam – it will cost you dearly.

GET THIS:
IF THE IMPORTANT IS IGNORED,
IT QUICKLY BECOMES A CRISIS

3 *The Monthly Medal*

John, a good club scratch player, saw Gus the circus gorilla hit a golfball three to four hundred yards, clean as a whistle, straight as a die, every time! John was extremely impressed and asked Gus to partner him in the club championship four ball. The unlikely pairing attracted some attention. The large gallery was amazed when the gorilla struck the ball off the first tee 380 yards straight into the heart of the green and three feet past the pin. The pair strode onto the green with some confidence and Gus, left with a relatively easy uphill putt, casually took out his putter, lined up his putt and, with a perfect swing, slammed the ball 300 yards back up the fairway!

SO YOU THINK YOU'VE GOT IT ...

In life we can get locked into predictable patterns of behaviour. A little finesse is a help. There are always at least two options available to us: what is predictable and what is possible. The most important six inches in golf is the six inches between your ears. Stop being a gorilla, use your head, try to explore options other than your normal behaviour and open up to all the possibilities. You may even end up with a medal.

GET THIS:
INSANITY IS DOING THE SAME THING OVER AND OVER AND EXPECTING A DIFFERENT RESULT

4 To Sweat or to Swan

A cabinet minister working sixteen hours a day and making great progress on the outer journey came to Gandhi one day and said, 'Gandhi, I'm totally exhausted, I'm working all the hours God gave me and I haven't an ounce of energy left. I am stressed out of my mind. What can I do?'

Gandhi said, 'Take fifteen minutes to yourself during the day and meditate.'

The minister retorted, 'Gandhi, you are completely missing the point, you have no idea how busy I am, that's just impossible!'

Gandhi replied, 'Well in that case you better take thirty minutes.'

SO YOU THINK YOU'VE GOT IT ...

Working harder is not the solution, it is the problem. The most useful activity in personal or organisational life often starts with inactivity and the use to which that apparent inactivity is put. Slow down, distance yourself from the problem, think clearly and take appropriate action. If that does not work then reflect on why that may be so.

GET THIS:
WORK SMARTER NOT HARDER

5 Blissful Ignorance

Sally, a bright, young, carefree swallow had just enjoyed her first eight months in Ireland: a beautiful spring, a glorious summer, and a mild autumn. The onset of a cold harsh winter was something she had not yet experienced. Experienced swallows knew you couldn't survive an Irish winter and so her parents told her it was time to leave.

Swallow after swallow left, but nothing would persuade Sally to go. Her parents pleaded and waited, waited and pleaded, until Sally was the last swallow to leave the telegraph wires. It was a bitterly cold morning as Sally set out on the long journey south. The further she went the heavier she felt as her wings began to freeze over. Eventually, she could flap them no more. She plummeted to the ground but fortunately fell into a cowpat which broke her fall. Dazed, shocked, tired, frozen and now this, up to her neck in cow manure! Oh, how she wished she had listened to her mother and father! She broke down in tears.

As luck would have it, the heat of the cowpat started slowly to melt the ice. Her body thawed, her wings freed up and she began to sing with delight. A passing hawk heard her, swooped down and plucked her out of the cowpat, washed her and ate her for lunch.

5 *Blissful Ignorance*

There are some people who will not take advice; they think they know it all, especially if all their experiences to date are positive. Oscar Wilde said, 'to give advice is foolish, to give good advice is absolutely fatal'. He could well have said, 'to ignore advice is foolish, to ignore good advice is absolutely fatal'. If, by chance, as you go through life you happen to land in the manure, keep your mouth shut and don't draw unnecessary attention to yourself, for those who help you are – more often than not – doing it out of self-interest.

> **GET THIS:**
> **ALMOST ANYTHING IS EASIER GOT INTO THAN OUT OF**

6 *Flashy But Flummoxed*

The first car I was in a position to choose – rather than the one I had to buy because of financial constraints – was a yellow Capri. God, it was a smashing car: slim lines, bright colours, an attention grabber.

Dating was simple, not because of any prowess on my part but because of the attention paid to my yellow Capri. Many Saturday nights I arranged to go out with women from North County Dublin but I would only half hear their address and directions because my mind was preoccupied with other thoughts. North County Dublin is a maze of narrow unsigned roads and there are no indications which are the primary roads and which are the secondary ones. I would often drive up to a junction, look left and right, make a hurried choice based on insufficient information and accelerate away from it like the clappers. As dusk fell the landscape would become increasingly unfamiliar. In a panic I would speed up and inevitably arrive at my destination dishevelled, ungrounded and invariably late.

SO YOU THINK YOU'VE GOT IT . . .

When people are lost or confused they tend to panic and demand action, often any action. They are lost but making up for it with speed.

Sometimes you have to slow down and admit you are lost before you can make progress. The necessity to

6 *Flashy But Flummoxed*

think and reflect on the situation before deciding on the proper course of action is paramount. As the song in *Oliver* goes, 'I'm reviewing the situation, I think I need to think it out again'.

> GET THIS:
> SPEED IS ONLY GOOD IF LED BY WISDOM

7 *The Jarveys*

Two tourists sitting on a pony and trap in Killarney were discussing the unique charm of the Irish character. One had observed that you could never get a straight answer to a direct question from anybody in Ireland. The second thought that was a bit harsh and stated that was not his experience. To prove his point he walked over to two jarveys sitting on the window ledge of the local post office. 'Could you tell me where the nearest post office is?' he asked.

'Would it be stamps you're looking for?' replied the jarvey.

SO YOU THINK YOU'VE GOT IT ...

Getting solid, accurate information doesn't always come easily. A meaningless conversation based on two people asking one another questions can go on forever. The break-through to exchange of relevant information takes place when a relationship has been developed and the fragile issue of trust has been resolved. This takes time.

In the business world people like to short circuit time where possible because 'time is money' but the currency for good quality information is both time and money. In this case, those seeking the information would have received a more satisfactory answer if they had invested time in building a relationship.

GET THIS:
RELATIONSHIP 1ST, INFORMATION 2ND

8 To Hammer the Point Home

Charlie, a carpet layer by profession, and a good husband, did not believe in the adage, 'You never see a cobbler with a good pair of shoes or a tailor in a fine suit'. Charlie was house-proud, hated wooden floors and liked to please his loving wife Bernie.

He had a long-standing arrangement with Bernie to lay a new sitting room carpet for their twenty-fifth wedding anniversary. As good as his word, on Saturday afternoon Charlie did his usual professional job. When finished, he stood up, wiped the sweat from his brow and, dying for a smoke, reached into his back pocket for his cigarettes. While searching the room with his eyes he called out to Bernie, 'Have you seen my cigarettes?' To his horror, just then he noticed a bulge in the middle of the carpet at the far end of the room. 'Blast,' he muttered and he moved quickly to rectify the situation before Bernie appeared. Rather than lift the whole carpet he beat out the bulge, moved what was left towards the skirting board and quickly re-tacked the carpet. 'A man on a galloping horse wouldn't notice the difference and anyhow the two-seater couch will be going there,' he noted.

Just then Bernie came through the door, 'Charlie, I've found your cigarettes,' she warmly exclaimed, 'but you won't believe it, the canary has gone missing!'

8 To Hammer the Point Home

It is better to know exactly what you are trying to put right before you try to fix it. The presenting problem and the real problem can be very different. Men who attend the doctor characteristically present a minor problem first; not to test the doctor's competence but to open the door to a discussion on what they fear may be a more complex one. The more indefinable the problem appears, the more cautious your response should be towards solving it. Be wary of taking a shot in the dark. You may well do untold damage and put yourself in a position where you are unable to retrieve the situation.

GET THIS:
A SHOT IN THE DARK IS
BEST LEFT TO FUNFAIRS

Chapter 2
A Rut or a Route

9 Extra Curricular Activity

John's school results had been in steady decline but worse still, he was showing signs of behavioural difficulties. The teacher decided to grasp the nettle and send for his parents. 'John is basically a good kid,' she began, 'but I am beginning to have great difficulty trusting him. As soon as anybody turns their back he will compulsively steal something – their pen, a ruler, a textbook – whatever comes easily to hand.'

Flabbergasted, his father replied, 'I just can't understand that; if I've told him once I've told him a thousand times, I can get any of that stuff from the office.'

SO YOU THINK YOU'VE GOT IT ...

Just as a picture paints a thousand words, people's deeds have a far more powerful impact on us than their words or intentions. People are motivated by example and what they see going on around them. If there is a lack of congruence between the spoken word and the ensuing action they will always choose the action as their guide. Example and modelling instil the values and demonstrate the behaviour the culture demands. The future is born out of the present.

GET THIS:
EXAMPLE IS THE BEST TEACHER

10 *Hard Labour*

Benny, a Dubliner, a working man, true to his craft and to his class, knew both the price and the value of things. Throughout his life he had worked his way up the ranks of his company and his beloved union. Not a man to tolerate fools lightly, he had proudly achieved what he had by the sweat of his brow and not by being a nuisance. No poacher turned gamekeeper was he!

Benny was now head of the union branch and was deeply respected in the industrial relations field with a reputation as a negotiator without equal. He was negotiating the final pay agreement for his members and wanted to leave them the best deal possible as his legacy.

There was the usual tough bargaining, banging on the table, temper tantrums, hard won inches, eventual agreement and then on to the ritual transparent consultation with branch members. After several rounds of negotiation Benny agreed a deal way beyond anything he could have reasonably expected. He called a meeting of the branch members to rubber stamp the agreement. He addressed them as follows: 'Brothers, after years of sacrifice and tireless commitment to this company and on the back of your hard work and steadfast resolve, we have finally arrived at an outcome which recognises the part you, and indeed your families, have played in making this company what it is today: a prosperous company, generating huge profits, with excellent labour relations and a secure future. As a result of your endeavours I was able to negotiate an agreement without precedent in the history of the trade union movement. I am proud to inform you that henceforth, with your approval, you will only have to work one day a week and that is on a Saturday!'

A dissenting but recognisable voice was raised instantly at the back of the canteen. It was Joe, who jumped to his feet and angrily shouted to Benny at the top table: 'Hold on a minute, do you mean every Saturday?'

<blockquote>SO YOU THINK YOU'VE GOT IT …</blockquote>

A wise and workable solution is not one that is imposed and reflected in the cliché 'It is my way or the highway'. John Hume, the Nobel Peace Prize winner, observed, 'Victory is not a solution'. If you want commitment to an agreement, all sides need to be happy with the outcome, with something in it for everyone. These are called win/win agreements and are particularly difficult to construct. They are the very antithesis of winner-take-all and can only be obtained if the bargaining parties are prepared to listen to one another and are willing to give a little in the interest of finding a solution which will improve relationships into the future.

> GET THIS:
> SOME PEOPLE JUST CANNOT TAKE 'YES'
> FOR AN ANSWER

11 The Pair on the Ground

Two people were standing in the National Gallery in Merrion Square, Dublin, studying a beautiful painting of the Garden of Eden. The first person, a Russian, said, 'Adam and Eve must be Russian, look they have only one apple and they are sharing it – true socialists.'

'No, no, no!' said his companion, a French tourist. 'They are French, see how happy they are, naked, staring into each other's eyes and about to make passionate love.'

'Not at all,' said the passing curator, a Dubliner born and bred, 'They are definitely Irish, look, they have no money, no clothes, nothing to drink, nothing to eat but an apple and they still think they are in Heaven!'

SO YOU THINK YOU'VE GOT IT ...

Culture hugely influences perspective, and perspective influences understanding and your capacity to take action. If you want to understand how deep rooted and controlling culture truly is, live in a different culture and try to change it. Some people would have us believe the apple on the tree was the cause of original sin. Others are adamant it wasn't, it was the pair on the ground. Now try changing that! Einstein believed you have to know something to change it, but many are equally convinced you only get to know something when you try to change it. In life, change is inevitable and growth is optional. When it comes to personal growth you have two choices: you can either think yourself into a new way of acting or act yourself into a new way of thinking. Either option is difficult because choosing growth can be counter cultural and at odds with those around you.

> **GET THIS:**
> **PERSONAL GROWTH OFTEN REQUIRES LEAVING THE TRIBE**

12 *Get Smart*

From childhood, Seamus O'Flynn wanted to join the CIA or MI5 as an agent; a job requiring intelligence, total commitment and loyalty. He was youthful, had great energy and liked to focus on completing the task, no matter what the odds. He was a high achiever. During the recruitment process to the intelligence services he was handed a gun and told to kill the person in the next room: the loyalty test. He duly headed into the next room to follow his instructions.

All hell broke loose. There was screaming and roaring, grunting and groaning, thuds and thumps, tables and chairs crashing against the walls with no respite. This went on for fifty minutes. Eventually Seamus emerged, blood splattered, dishevelled, clothes all but ripped off him and literally exhausted. He leaned against the table and looked the chairman of the assessment centre in the eyes and proclaimed triumphantly, 'Job done! But, boy was it tough, you guys need to get your act together, there were blanks in that gun!'

SO YOU THINK YOU'VE GOT IT ...

Beware of loyalty tests. Make sure they are ethical – very often they are not. Good judgement is a help but if you find yourself operating out of fear, something is radically wrong. We are sometimes asked to carry out really difficult tasks and are given neither the proper tools nor support to do the job. It is no wonder the job turns out messy and of doubtful value. Consequently the organisation generally attributes blame to the person who has carried out its instructions rather than looking at its own part in the whole affair.

> GET THIS:
> THE BOSS IS ON THE PODIUM FOR YOUR
> SUCCESS AND IN YOUR FACE FOR
> HIS FAILURE

13 Hair Styling by Ed

Edward always had his hair cut (whether it needed to be or not) on the first Saturday of the month. He preferred to call it hair*styled* for he had become fastidious in his early teens when he first began to notice women. He was a stylist in everything he did: his clothes had style, his car had style and he played squash with style. Everything to him was a statement. He was well educated, clean-shaven, wore contact lenses and had a spotted handkerchief in his breast pocket. A respectable banker and son of a doctor he was destined for the top.

On the first Saturday of every month, daring, adventure and the expression of individuality took over: no wash, cut and blow-dry for him but a new hairstyle. A tint, a highlight, a brand mark, just to finish it off, the subtlest of changes but changes nevertheless. Fashion and style don't stand still and he abhorred the admonishments of his squash mates: 'There is only a fortnight between a bad haircut and a good one!'

It was the first Saturday in May and traditionally Edward got a little more hair off with his summer styling. After the wash he sat in the chair and Monica excitedly awaited her latest instructions, for Edward was always a challenge to her craft. 'Monica will you use a number one blade on the right hand side of my head, remove the lock and all the hair except the fringe over my forehead. I want you to zig-zag the fringe like forked lightning, but leave it one inch longer on the

13 Hair Styling by Ed

right side than on the left. Under no circumstances alter the length of my left lock but just straighten the line below the ear lobe. Above the ear I want two parallel lines from back to front like tram tracks: the Luas look! I want you to leave a little tail at the back just like the Mohican Indians and you can plait it for effect, but that's optional. On the crown of my head, just left of centre, I want you to cut out an octagonal shape like the old fifty pence piece, only bigger. Finally blow dry it left to right to cover some of the bald patches and put a hint of conditioner on to keep what's left in place.'

Monica, amazed at the request and wishing to save Edward the embarrassment and inevitable public humiliation from such an onslaught on his hair, exclaimed in horror, 'Edward, I don't think I can do that!'

'Of course you can Monica,' he replied, 'that's what you did the last time I was in here.'

SO YOU THINK YOU'VE GOT IT ...

Accountability and ownership go hand in hand. In problem-solving the question you should most frequently ask is, 'Who owns the problem', for inevitably they will have a major say in its resolution. If you delegate responsibility you need to be very clear on what you expect and what the intended outcomes are. You either have confidence in those to whom you delegated the responsibility

13 *Hair Styling by Ed*

or you haven't – either way you are accountable. If you haven't complete confidence in their ability you better sweat now and supervise the detail. If not, you'll certainly sweat later and you may indeed be on your way to a public hanging.

> GET THIS:
> YOU GET WHAT YOU INSPECT, NOT WHAT YOU EXPECT

14 A Committed Northsider

When asked why, as a true blue Dublin northsider, I had moved to the southside of the city, I told the story of a friend of mine: grounded, rich, happy, two houses, three cars, four racehorses, five children. He woke up one morning feeling a bit down and insecure. He turned to his wife and said, 'Darling, if I hadn't all the money I have, and if I wasn't a success in the eyes of our friends, and if I couldn't keep you in the manner to which you are accustomed, would you still love me?'

She replied, 'You are the nicest, kindest, most compassionate man I ever met! Don't be ridiculous; of course I would still love you. I would miss you but I would still love you!'

I could today be living on the northside, still loved and sadly missed.

SO YOU THINK YOU'VE GOT IT ...

You cannot step boldly into the future while looking over your shoulder – live in the present! Don't look back unless you can smile, don't look forward unless you can dream and don't dwell on fundamental questions about the past or the future when you are feeling insecure; it is self destructive.

GET THIS:
LIVE IN THE PRESENT; IT IS A GIFT

15 *An Eagle or an Albatross*

Johnny found an eagle's egg and put it in the nest of a barnyard hen. Time passed, the eagle hatched with the brood of chickens and grew up with them.

All his life, Eddie the Eagle, thinking he was a barnyard chicken, did what the barnyard chickens did. He cackled and clucked, he scratched the earth for worms and insects, and in moments of real adventure, he thrashed his wings and flew a few feet just above the ground. His 'mother' soon put an end to that nonsense and he became so sensible his mates nicknamed him Steady Eddie.

Years passed, his mother died, and the eagle grew very old. He even went bald. One day, he saw an amazing sight: a magnificent bird above him in the cloudless sky. It glided effortlessly in graceful majesty among the powerful wind currents with scarcely a beat of its strong golden wings.

Steady Eddie looked up in awe. 'Who's that?' he asked his mate, Chuck the Chicken. 'That's the eagle, the king of the birds,' said Chuck. 'He belongs to the sky, we belong to the earth, we're chickens.'

So Steady Eddie lived and died a chicken, for that's what he thought he was and was reared to be.

15 *An Eagle or an Albatross*

Self-belief and a positive self-image are essential components for success. If you know what you are, you know what to do. Listen to the tapes you play in your head, eject the negative ones and don't wait until you are too old or go grey to ask the right questions. Keeping your self-belief is hard work and requires total commitment as there are lots of people out there willing to rain on your parade and label you as ordinary.

GET THIS:
THE BEGINNING OF WISDOM IS TO CALL
THINGS BY THEIR RIGHT NAME

16 Caught Flat-Footed

Bridget, a country girl by name and nature, graduated from college and got her first job teaching English in Dublin's inner city. Being civic spirited and with a deep and firmly held view of what education was all about, Bridget gave her class, as one of its first tasks, an essay titled 'The Gardaí'. She asked the students on completion of the essay to put their biros down, fold their arms and remain quietly in their places. Happy in the knowledge that this would take at least a quarter of an hour Bridget began to prepare her lesson notes for the following day.

To her surprise, after a couple of minutes Jason, good natured but by no means the brightest star in the firmament, was sitting back, biro on desk, arms folded, chewing gum with a smug grin on his face – one of the few things he could do simultaneously. 'Jason, are you finished your essay?' enquired Bridget.

'Yes, miss,' he replied.

'Ok, stand up and read it out.'

Jason stood up and read out the following, 'The gardaí are bastards,' gave a bow, took a round of applause and sat down.

Bridget was horrified, especially as she was in a relationship with Simon, the community liaison garda in nearby Kevin Street. She immediately arranged with Simon to take her class to Kevin Street Station the following week to see at first hand how ordinary they were and how things worked in a garda station.

The kids' eyes popped at the sophisticated tracking devices, the rigour of systematic investigation, modern interrogation techniques and the information technology generated data. In fact, the gardaí seemed to know more about the whereabouts of the kids' fathers than the kids themselves. The kids went on patrol in the squad cars, used computer-guided navigation, two-way radios and linked up with other patrol cars at the scene of an investigation. The whole experience was very exciting and deemed a wonderful success. All in all a credit to experiential learning.

'Nothing like reinforcement though,' Bridget reflected, as she had a brainwave: she would give the class the same essay as last week. She went through her well-practised routine. The essay, 'The Gardaí'. 'When you are finished put your biro down, fold your arms and sit quietly in your place.' Not altogether surprised that Jason was more thoughtful this time, but nevertheless amazed at how quickly he had finished, Bridget called him to the top of the class. She was hopeful of great things to come as Jason had got on famously with the gardaí on the school outing. 'Jason, read out your essay to the class.'

'Yes, miss,' he replied, as polite as ever. Drawing himself up to his full height, Jason read out the following, 'The gardaí are cute bastards,' and took a bow to tumultuous applause.

16 *Caught Flat-Footed*

Rote learning and experiential learning have their place in adult education, but a health warning needs to be attached to both. Rote learning leaves nothing to the imagination, experiential learning everything. Boundaries need to be explored and a context agreed; if not, people will contextualise the learning themselves and you may indeed end up like Bridget, dumbfounded. The fortune teller with the sign on his door announcing, 'closed this afternoon due to unforeseen circumstances' didn't see what was coming either.

GET THIS:
MANAGE THE CONTEXT AND MINIMISE
THE SURPRISES

Chapter 3

Blackspots or Goosebumps

Hanging on by Your Fingertips

A man on a solitary walk up the Dublin mountains loses his footing and slides fifty yards down and over a cliff. He throws his hands out, clawing at the soil and manages to grab a branch of an overhanging tree, stopping miraculously. Dangling and terrified, he screams for help. 'Is there anybody up there?' he cries.

'Yes,' answers a voice, 'and I will help you.'

He sighs and calls out with relief, 'Hurry! Hurry! The branch is breaking under my weight.'

'Let go of the branch,' the voice on the cliff top says, 'and you will float like a feather down to the bottom of the gorge.'

'Who are you?' shouts the man in total disbelief.

'I am God, the source of all compassion, kindness, caring and love.'

The man ponders for a moment, looks up at the cliff top once more and cries out in complete panic, 'Is there anybody else up there?'

SO YOU THINK YOU'VE GOT IT ...

The opportunity of a lifetime has to be grasped within the lifetime of the opportunity. An offer too good to be true does not stay on the table forever. Some things have to be taken on trust. Good managers create an environment of trust and optimism, a belief that things can and will be better. Poor managers are incredibly powerful also, for their work results in despair, hopelessness and a blanket of pessimism being thrown over the organisation. To build a belief that things can and will be better takes courage and integrity because the creation of false hope and unfulfilled expectations does more harm than good.

> GET THIS:
> NOTHING CAN BE ACHIEVED WITHOUT
> FAITH, ESPECIALLY MIRACLES

18 Shooting Yourself in the Foot

Tommy Gunne, known for his quick fire temperament, was stopped by the gardaí for speeding. The garda said to Tommy, 'You were driving in excess of 130 kilometres per hour and furthermore you were reckless: you crossed the continuous white line on several occasions.'

Tommy quickly retorted, 'Excuse me, garda, I have been travelling these roads for years and I was doing less than 100 kilometres per hour.'

The garda didn't like his authority being questioned, 'I don't want any guff from you, I have it on the record and I have my co-driver as a witness: 130 kilometres an hour is what you were doing and you were reckless!'

'Look garda, I'm five kilometres from home, I've been driving these roads all my life and at no stage was I doing above 100 kilometres per hour. You may have been driving recklessly at 130 kilometres per hour trying to catch me but I know what speed I was doing, I was doing 100 kilometres.'

'My good man,' said the garda, 'I don't like your attitude and if you continue in that vein you'll be spending the night in a cell.' Exasperated, Tommy turned to his wife and asked her to speak up.

At that, Tommy's wife intervened. She leaned across and spoke to the garda, 'I am sorry about this, Tommy's normally very polite but when he has a couple of jars on him he becomes totally obnoxious.'

18 Shooting Yourself in the Foot

There are times when discretion is the better part of valour and you are better off owning up and taking what's coming to you. Be sure of the help you are enlisting and don't shoot yourself in the foot. Those who try to help you when you are in the wrong generally make the situation worse and you end up in a double bind. You lose the argument and you lose your friends.

GET THIS:
WHEN YOU ARE IN A HOLE,
STOP DIGGING

19 *A Wooden Heart*

It was early summer, a beautiful day, nothing to be heard in the farmyard but the cackle of the hens and the occasional barking of the solitary, retired work-dog, who still had visions of past glories. The oak tree stood majestically at the front of the house, where it had stood unperturbed for sixty years, embracing the shadow of the veranda. The rustle of the leaves accompanied the singing of the thrushes on the upper branches. All was well and the world was at peace. Alex the Axe, waking from a prolonged hibernation and facing the summer's work made his way to the large oak in a half-rolling, half-sauntering gait.

He called out bluntly, 'You, oak tree! You have many branches, I lost my handle last autumn, give me one of your sturdy branches.'

The oak tree benignly agreed.

Alex the Axe replaced his handle with the sturdy branch, and came back two days later and gleefully chopped down the mighty oak.

SO YOU THINK YOU'VE GOT IT ...

To be brought down to earth is bad enough, but to be brought down to earth by your own foolishness is both careless and painful. Too often out of kindness, naivety or fear, we collude in our own downfall. To be felled in the cut and thrust of life is one thing but to joyfully

19 *A Wooden Heart*

dance to somebody else's tune is sad, and the pain of that memory lasts well beyond the pain of the downfall. Often the best option is to say no straight away, for the key to failure is to try to please everybody.

> GET THIS:
> ## STAY SMART, EVEN WHEN DOING A GOOD TURN

20 *The Bear Necessities*

My brothers and I went bear-hunting in the Canadian Rockies some years ago. We had all the gear: a four wheel drive, flack jackets, binoculars, rifles, tents, sleeping bags, gas stoves and toothbrushes. Nothing was left to chance.

Somewhat inexperienced, we drove for six hours and as dusk was falling we came to a fork in the road. A sign read 'Bear Left'. Our courage was beginning to wane and I, being the junior, timidly suggested to my brother, 'that's it, no sense in us staying, even the bears have gone'.

He replied, 'Hold on a minute, we can't go home now, what will people say? Come hell or high water I'm going to get a bear skin coat.'

Two hours later, as we were setting up camp for the night, I saw my hardy eldest brother getting into his sleeping bag wearing, of all things, his Nike runners. 'What are you doing?' I enquired.

'If a bear comes across our camp tonight I need to be able to run,' he answered.

'Have you learned nothing?' I replied, 'Don't you know well you will never outrun a bear?'

'I don't have to outrun the bear,' he replied. 'All I have to do is outrun you'.

20 *The Bear Necessities*

The organisation is there to look after the needs of the organisation and in the final analysis it always will. Over-dependency on the organisation is neither healthy nor wise; in times of survival you are obliged to protect yourself. Organisations may have a culture but they rarely have a conscience. More often than not they have big brothers with their feet firmly on the career ladder, willing to carry out unquestioningly the company's practices, policies and procedures at your expense and do so to further their careers.

GET THIS:
TRUST NOBODY, NOT EVEN
YOUR BIG BROTHER

21 *Maverick*

A young salesman from Dublin walked into a pub for his lunch in the West of Ireland and was amazed to see a dog, know locally as Maverick, playing poker with three old men. The Dub sauntered over to the table and nonchalantly enquired, 'Can that dog really read cards?'

'Yes, but he is not much of a poker player,' replied one of the men in a dismissive low-key voice.

'Why is that?' asked the persistent Dub.

'Well whenever he gets a good hand, he wags his tail!' was the smug reply.

SO YOU THINK YOU'VE GOT IT ...

Brian Lenihan, the former government minister, once said to a successful candidate at a selection convention who was celebrating at the bar with his friends: 'If I were you I would go back into the hall to build bridges rather than be seen out here celebrating.' There is a thin line between being seen to succeed and being seen to be arrogant. Most people's success is at the expense of somebody else's failure but it is not necessary to rub people's noses in it. The pinnacle of one achievement is often the foundation stone for the next but the journey is not always simple and relationships can become frayed. Reconciliation is eased if you haven't wagged your tail.

GET THIS:
IT'S OK TO SUCCEED, BUT DON'T GLOAT

22 Lady Marlborough's Cat

Lady Marlborough loved to spend the month of June on the ritual London social circle: Royal Ascot, Wimbledon, garden parties, high fashion, strawberries and cream. She was the cream, didn't need to rise to the top; she was there by birth, a woman of substance, breeding and blue blood.

Lady Marlborough called the manor frequently to ensure all was right with the world, her world, the Estate. On Tuesday, the opening day of Royal Ascot, she got a call from Oscar, her new head butler; he had come highly recommended straight from Windsor Castle, a wonderful training ground. 'My lady,' Oscar informed her immediately, 'The west wing of the mansion is ablaze and the raging fire is not yet under control.' But Oscar, as always, was. 'Furthermore, your ladyship,' Oscar calmly informed her, 'Fluffy your cat is dead, he jumped from the roof to his death in the ensuing panic.'

Lady Marlborough was shocked into silence – a rare occurrence – but as with all well-bred west country ladies, she quickly regained her composure: 'Oscar, you are newly employed in my service,' she stated, 'and I would like to give you a word of advice that will stand you in good stead. I have a weak heart. It comes from my father's side of the family and is exacerbated when I get a shock. I would appreciate in future if you would recount such disasters as you have just conveyed to me somewhat more delicately. I suggest you could inform

22 Lady Marlborough's Cat

me that Fluffy, my beloved late husband's favourite cat, was out playing on the roof of the west wing. You saw him climbing into the master bedroom through the open window. He got caught in the draped curtains, panicked and pulled them off the wall. They hit the chandelier in the middle of the bedroom which fell on the dresser, knocked over the lighted candles and set the drapes on fire. The fire spread quickly and is out of control, the fire brigade has arrived and is having difficulty with the water pressure. The blaze has taken hold and the cat is nowhere to be seen. Have you got that Oscar? No bad news all at once please, for medical reasons.'

'Yes, my lady,' replied the slightly chastened Oscar, in a most polite, respectful, yet assured tone.

'Good,' replied Lady Marlborough. 'Before I put down the phone may I enquire about the well being of my mother, the Right Honourable Duchess of Dorchester?'

'Well, right at this moment, my lady, she is out on the roof of the west wing playing with Fluffy the cat,' was the sanguine reply.

22 Lady Marlborough's Cat

There are three types of feedback: meaningful, mischievous and malicious. A critic once said of Wagner's music, 'It's not as bad as it sounds' – mischievous or malicious? In spite of an abundance of training, people find it very difficult to give meaningful feedback. Conventional wisdom has it that feedback should be presented like a good sandwich: a palatable bit at both ends with the meaty bit in the middle. A formula that is all too predictable perhaps and known to both parties. A better option is to be honest, to keep the good of the recipients at the centre of the discussion, and don't overload them with data. You've got to focus on the fire, not the fluffy stuff, for it will all come out in the wash eventually.

> GET THIS:
> WHEN GIVING FEEDBACK, SEE IT ALL,
> IGNORE A LOT AND ACT ON A LITTLE

23 *Two's Company*

A romantic couple entered a high-class restaurant on their first date. On being shown to their table and given the menu, they noticed a rhinoceros sitting opposite them in the darkened corner of the restaurant. All night the staff and other clients ignored the rhino. The couple was too embarrassed to say anything to each other or to anyone else. They tried to eat their meal as if things were perfectly normal, each silently wondering what would happen if the rhino was disturbed. Should they dare bring it up with each other or with the restaurant staff? They finally left the restaurant distracted and oblivious to the good food and fine wine they had left on the table.

SO YOU THINK YOU'VE GOT IT ...

Sometimes the shadow side has to be addressed, just because it is there. If not, it gets in the way of the primary purpose. The rhino wasn't spoken about but he was part of the conversation. The couple was fearful that if inappropriately disturbed he could inflict untold damage. He certainly ruined the meal, the conversation and the night out because he was not dealt with in the restaurant. He followed the couple home, sat on the couch between them and got in the way of their primary purpose without saying a word.

GET THIS:
DEAL WITH THE BAGGAGE OR IT WILL COME BACK TO HAUNT YOU

24 *A Steward's Enquiry*

Mickey O'Donnell, a Clareman, loved horses; thoroughbreds had been part of his life and a family passion for decades. He trained one occasionally to fill the hole in his income and to meet the demands of the taxman when necessary.

In recent years he had a promising five-year-old mare called Rosie, who was in the form of her life and ready to defy the wily handicapper. A major coup and the winning of serious money was meticulously planned for Listowel in September, at a time when non-triers were asked to line up at the back. Even the children's piggy banks had been raided in anticipation of the big day.

Mickey and his nephew, a seven-pound claiming apprentice, were seen talking animatedly to one another in the parade ring, while the rest of the family was hanging on their every word. The moment arrived when young Sean Brown was legged up and mounted Rosie. As he completed the compulsory one circuit of the parade ring, Mickey nervously adjusted the bit in the horse's mouth, took something from his pocket and fed it to his beloved mare. The shrewd Lord Bonnybrook, the acting steward of the day, had been taking a keen interest in the proceedings. He approached Mickey, praised him on the condition of his horse and off-handedly enquired into the nature of the substance he had just given Rosie.

Mickey politely informed Lord Bonnybrook that the horse was more a family pet than a racehorse and greatly relaxed on the big occasion when fed the occasional sugar lump. In the midst of this conversation Mickey casually popped one into his mouth and kindly offered a lump to the surprised Lord Bonnybrook, who graciously accepted.

Mickey then took his leave of Lord Bonnybrook, went over towards Rosie as she neared the exit of the parade ring for the second time and emphasised again his instructions to young Sean from Kilrush: 'Come out of the starting stalls quickly, get a handy position four or five back, come into the straight wide to avoid interference, kick for home and with one run hit the front at the two furlong marker and you won't be caught! If anything passes you from behind it will be either Lord Bonnybrook or myself.'

SO YOU THINK YOU'VE GOT IT …

Thinking outside the box and quick-wittedness will get you out of many a tight corner. Creativity and innovation are the hallmarks of these attributes which are constantly in demand in organisations.

Two dominant cultures permeate an organisation: a proof culture and a belief culture. To thrive, creativity requires an investment in belief, not proof. If you have difficulty with belief you may have to trust the necessity under which other people operate. Because of the de-

24 *A Steward's Enquiry*

mands innovation and creativity make on the organisation to change, they are always under scrutiny. Management seemingly craves genius and talent yet at the same time wants it to behave like everyone else and so measures it accordingly. For genius and talent to flourish however, it often interprets these measurements liberally, which some might suggest is cheating.

> GET THIS:
> CREATIVITY THRIVES ON
> LIBERAL THINKING

Chapter 4

Defining Moments

A bullock got stuck in the ditch one day. We tried everything to get him out; we even tied ropes around him and tried to haul him out with the tractor. Nothing worked. Eventually, Tommy Daly, a wise and loyal herdsman who had worked on the farm for years, jumped into the ditch, leaned over the bullock's head, cupped his hands and let an almighty roar into the bullock's ear. The startled bullock struggled to his feet and clambered out of the ditch. Tommy smilingly commented, 'Sometimes, the best help you can give is to scare the living daylights out of them!'

SO YOU THINK YOU'VE GOT IT ...

Staff are seen as a resource, a cost or a liability. They will be whatever you expect them to be. Farmhands were never literally farmhands only; they were always both a physical and intellectual resource with generations of experience and wisdom behind them. Doctorates have been conferred on people who have written on organisational interventions, resistance to change and the depths of the intervention required to influence and move things forward. None was ever as revealing to me as the message bellowed into the bullock's ear that day.

GET THIS:
WITH EVERY PAIR OF HANDS YOU HIRE YOU GET A FREE HEAD

26 *Lively Lilly*

My Auntie Lilly, a Dundalk woman, died at 96 years of age without ever having been sick. Shortly before she died I asked her, 'Of all the changes that you've seen in your lifetime what has amazed you most?' She dwelt on the question for several minutes and finally answered, 'When I was young, all the nuns were cooped up and the hens were free range, now all the nuns are free range and the hens are cooped up.'

SO YOU THINK YOU'VE GOT IT ...

Ageism is rampant as are other 'ism's. Our assumptions must be questioned, for we bring our own biases to each encounter; we listen only with tired ears and we hear only what we expect. The medium and the message are not the same thing. The older people are the more they become sensitive to technological change and its impact on their lives. Their environment has been threatened by mobile phones, ipods and laptops, the subsequent loss of a sense of community, and the isolation experienced through the disconnection between people. As a result, the elderly often express their social commentary through storytelling and imagery which may be too easily dismissed as old fashioned, irrelevant or just plain boring.

GET THIS:
MATURE REFLECTION IS NOT
INSTANTANEOUS

27 Himself and the Brother

Himself and the brother met for a jar in the local on Thursday nights. The first pint was always accompanied by an exchange of views on the family and how they were making out. Times were hard, it was the 1950s, Ireland was in recession and they were both unemployed. Depression, they would prefer to call it, but that cut too close to the bone.

One pint followed another and as they became more lubricated their imaginations took flight and himself and the brother got around to the issues of the day. The more complex the topic the more certain became the solution, for himself had a great mind and the brother was well practised in prompting it. Tonight the Irish economy took centre stage. Though admirers of Eamon de Valera, the taoiseach, his apparent lack of foresight in taking a neutral stance and not entering the Second World War on the Allied side, bemused them. As Ireland had remained neutral, it was unable to take advantage of the Marshall Plan and the generosity of the United States to both victors and vanquished.

Following the train of his own thought as he often did, for to quote an authority on such matters, 'How do I know what I'm thinking until I hear myself say it', himself says to the brother: 'If we declared war on the United States we could solve all our problems!'

'You think?' replies the brother.

'I've no doubt,' says himself with increasing confidence

and a certain quickening of the monologue. 'They would beat the living daylights out of us and if past performance is anything to go by they will feel guilty, shower us with millions of dollars, reconstruct everything they have destroyed, provide cheap healthcare, free education and give everyone a job. Even if I say so myself, it's a master stroke, we would be wiped out in a couple of days and the rebuilding could take place straight away.'

The brother, dumbstruck by the audacity of it all, paused deep in thought, took a long, thoughtful gulp from his pint, rubbed the white of the pint head from his lips and enquired of himself, 'And what if we won?'

SO YOU THINK YOU'VE GOT IT ...

There is no situation so bad that a skilled worrier cannot make it worse. The pessimist asks, 'what if?' the optimist, 'what now?' Both characteristics are essential to life and organisations, but not in equal measure. Listen to yourself and if the question is exclusively, 'what now', you are not giving the issue enough consideration. If the question is exclusively, 'what if', events are getting far too much consideration and nothing is happening. Worse still, you may be typecast as a hopeless case and end up unemployed with nobody to talk to except the brother.

GET THIS:
DOOMSDAY IS EVERYDAY FOR SOME

28 *The Gun Dogs*

A neighbour of mine bred and trained pedigree gun dogs; he placed the following advertisement in the British sports magazine *Country Life*:

PEDIGREE GUN DOGS FOR SALE

One: A highly trained top class dog for £1,500 sterling

Two: A nearly-trained dog with lots of potential for £900 sterling

Three: A young dog with good pedigree and a fast learner for £500 sterling

He had just made a sale to Lady Ashford in Berkshire.

'Which dog did she buy?' I enquired.

'The only one I had!' he replied.

SO YOU THINK YOU'VE GOT IT …

Everyone lives by selling something. What they are selling and what they say they are selling are often two different things. Buyer beware! Beware of dogs and certainly don't buy a pup from one! Rigorous questioning is a necessary first step in the purchasing process and it isn't a bad idea to examine the papers thoroughly, especially if you are paying pedigree prices!

GET THIS:
YOU CAN SELL ANYTHING, YOU CAN ONLY DELIVER ON WHAT YOU'VE GOT

29 *The Mule Train*

I was at the Grand Canyon last September and while there I noticed a large mule train at the bottom of the gorge, winding its way slowly but relentlessly upwards. I watched for more than two hours and reflected on the fact that the lead mule was the only one who ever got a change of scenery. At the same time I imagined the panic that would ensue if the mule in the middle got pig-headed and stubbornly refused to move.

It is almost impossible to be outstanding without standing out. You are seen either to lead or to lag, to take a position on issues or not. Lester Piggott, the legendary jockey said, 'It is not good enough to have a position in a horse race, you've got to own that position.' The question in today's collaborative and complex world is how can you be responsible and exercise appropriate authority by owning a leadership position while allowing sufficient space for other people's leadership and followership talents to emerge.

GET THIS:
LEAD, FOLLOW, OR GET OUT OF THE WAY

30 *The Fox and the Harvester*

One of the clearest memories of my childhood is sitting on the combine harvester watching the cutting of the corn. In the middle of the uncut corn was a stealthy fox who kept moving to the opposite side of the field away from the oncoming ruthless harvester. He would stick his nose out of the corn and calculate how far he had to run to make the ditch in safety. Every time he ran to the opposite side of the cornfield and looked out, we had cut another round of the field and the ditch was that much further away. His tempo quickened as the harvester closed in on him. He was panicking at the thought of getting stranded further from the safety of the ditch. When he was left with no option and was about to be swallowed up by the harvester he made a break for it, ran half the width of the field across open country to the welcome shelter of the ditch.

SO YOU THINK YOU'VE GOT IT ...

There is a difference between making decisions and exercising judgement. Judgement is most in demand when the choices seem equally balanced. When the weighing scales tips and the outcome seems obvious, a decision is easily made. You can have poor judgement and still delude yourself into thinking you are a good decision maker when all you are doing is choosing the inevitable.

GET THIS:
CHOOSING AND DECIDING ARE NOT THE SAME

31 A Simple Solution

John, tense, frustrated, bothered and angry, was seeking peace of mind. He had pursued both the usual courses of action and the unusual without success. In a final attempt to find tranquillity he went to the holy man on top of the mountain.

'Holy man,' he said, 'I'm looking for the gift of tranquillity and in a last, desperate attempt I have come to you. You are so content! How do you do it?'

The holy man thought for a moment, and said, 'I never disagree with anybody.'

'Ah, come off it!' reacted John. 'There's got to be more to it than that!'

The holy man reflected once again and replied, 'John, you are probably right.'

We frequently go to the holy man to seek answers, and are given simple, practical and profound advice, yet dismiss it out of hand. It is much more flattering to be given a complex diagnosis and a costly solution. The often trotted out answers conventional wisdom seems to agree upon require lots of graft, are nigh impossible to implement, and in the end doom you to failure.

GET THIS:
SIMPLE ADVICE CAN BE SIMPLY TOO
HARD TO FOLLOW

I had an uncle who was sick and in hospital once. At the end of visiting hours, I enquired of him, 'Would you like to go to the bathroom before I leave?'

'No,' he replied, 'but if you want me to, I will.'

SO YOU THINK YOU'VE GOT IT ...

The building of dependency can be a conscious or unconscious process. Either way it reduces the capacity of the individual to think and act for his/her self. Organisations and institutions are huge teaching machines. They teach the individual how and when to behave. We need to be careful not to unwittingly collude with the organisation in this subtle process of disempowerment. Compliance and creativity are unhappy bedfellows.

GET THIS: INSTITUTIONALISATION IS ABOUT COMPLIANCE

33 Gone Fishing

Granddad and his bright 25-year-old postgraduate grandson Tony went fishing together.

'Look at the fish, see how they are enjoying themselves,' said Granddad.

Tony replied, 'Granddad, you are not a fish, so how do you know they are enjoying themselves?'

'You are not me so how do you know I don't know they are enjoying themselves?' Granddad answered.

SO YOU THINK YOU'VE GOT IT ...

In Africa they say that with the passing of every old man a library burns down. Age brings maturity, vast experience, wisdom, insight and good judgement; sometimes we underestimate the depth of what is going on in older people's heads. We may have to accept not only that the old know more about being young than the young know about being old, but that they also bring huge experience to that. That experience may well be worth taking on trust for they have been baiting fish for a long time.

GET THIS:
YOU CANNOT HAVE OTHER
PEOPLE'S INSIGHTS

Chapter 5

Essence or Absence

34 *What Goes Around ...*

The priest, the minister and the rabbi were having an ecumenical drink one evening and the discussion led to the profound topic of 'life and when does life begin?'

The priest said with some certainty, 'at the moment of conception.'

The minister disputed that and said with equal authority, 'after sixteen weeks in the womb.'

The rabbi interjected and said, 'when your children move out and the dog dies.'

SO YOU THINK YOU'VE GOT IT ...

Most transformative learning is experienced, not taught. Winston Churchill commented, 'I loved learning, I hated being taught.' Application and reflection, action and thinking are the ingredients of healthy learning. Thinking and reflecting is hard work. To quote Oscar Wilde, 'Only the shallow know themselves.'

GET THIS:
THE REWARD OF SUFFERING
IS EXPERIENCE

35 *Getting Stung*

Tommy Daly, the farmhand, was full of old wisdom. When cleaning up a ditch with his bare hands, Tommy would grasp or choke the nettles and never get stung. He often invited me to do the same, but I never had the courage. He would clean up an area with great confidence and effectiveness, just like a sickle going through a meadow, and yet apparently suffer no pain.

> SO YOU THINK YOU'VE GOT IT ...

Henry Ford once said, 'whether you believe you can or you can't you are probably right!' There are two things that determine effectiveness: attitude and ability. Self belief, optimism and trust are the characteristics of a good attitude. Pessimism and mistrust rarely build anything. Ask the Wright brothers who built and flew the first plane. We all have the ability to grasp the nettle; it's just that when it comes to being stung, we are often pessimists.

> ### GET THIS:
> IF YOU GET STUNG, YOU PROBABLY DIDN'T HAVE ENOUGH SELF-BELIEF

I was recently asked to give advice to an introspective eighteen-year-old who was trying to make some crucial career choices. In desperation I finally asked, 'John, what would you really really like to do?'

'I'd like to be a U.S. Air Force pilot,' he said, ' but the idea of it would kill my mother, she would be horrified at the thought.'

'Look, John, it's your career, your future, not your mother's. Anyhow I'm sure she is perfectly reasonable, why don't you ask her?' I suggested.

'I can't,' said John, 'she died two years ago.'

SO YOU THINK YOU'VE GOT IT ...

Some people suffering from paralysis by analysis get overwhelmed and freeze with fear. In refusing to act, they subconsciously choose the certainty of misery over the misery of uncertainty. You cannot know for sure the answer until you ask the question. Better to die in an attempt to find out than to die wondering. Sometimes no one's permission is required to do something except your own. Be kind to yourself and remember at the end of the day that forgiveness is often easier got than permission.

GET THIS:
THE SHADOW OF AUTHORITY IS LONGER THAN THE ARM OF AUTHORITY

37 A Little Less Conversation

Vincent had been on the road for as long as he could remember. His current job as a salesman with a fertiliser company had brought two of his passions together: selling and contact with the rural community in the south of Ireland, many of whom, like himself, had a passionate interest in horses. To survive over the years he had adopted a certain code of practice or 'Rules of the Road' as he would call them. 'Restaurants for meals, hotels for beds and pubs for pints,' was one of his mantras. He didn't believe in eating a meal or drinking a pint without visiting the rest room, not to relieve himself but to inspect the premises. 'You'll not get a dirty loo and a clean kitchen,' he would say, 'and I cannot walk into the kitchen.'

He was a family man and whenever possible he would squeeze five days work into four and get home late on a Thursday night. As well as giving him a well-deserved three-day weekend, the extra cash he saved on the overnight expenses was a bonus to the family at Christmas.

Vincent worked late hours and was often playing catch-up. It was 7 p.m. and he found himself between jobs, between towns and in two minds. Good sense prevailed. Vincent decided to call it a day and headed to the nearest small rural town. As he approached the town he saw two lads holding up the gable end wall of a pub, drinking a pint and smoking a cigarette; 'multi-tasking' he called it. Unfamiliar with the town, he pulled up

37 *A Little Less Conversation*

parallel to the two lads and wound down his window. 'Is there a hotel in this town?' he asked.

'Two,' replied Pat Joe, the more verbose of the lads.

'Which one should I stay in?' enquired Vincent.

'It doesn't matter,' replied his by now new best friend.

'What do you mean it doesn't matter? I've done a hard day's work, am looking forward to a half decent meal, a good night's sleep and an early start in the morning.'

'It still doesn't matter,' said the other man. 'Whichever one you stay in, when you wake up in the morning you will wish you had stayed in the other one.'

SO YOU THINK YOU'VE GOT IT ...

Language is important, especially when you are living in a small, intimate community with the intention of staying there. You may not always call things as they are, but to live with yourself and others you don't have to call them as they are not. Truth and honesty are two different things. We can maintain our integrity by being loyal to the truth, it is how we tell it that often contains the pain for others and, ultimately, for ourselves. Pat Joe, if not the greatest conversationalist in the world, was wise, and loyal to the truth.

GET THIS:
TO BE TRUTHFUL AND NOT CAUSE
OFFENCE REQUIRES PRACTICE

38 *Join the Club*

Jesus was out for his usual Sunday morning stroll. Today he chose Birmingham, Alabama, a town deep in the southern part of the United States.

The streets were quiet. All that could be heard above the sound of autumn leaves dancing down the main street, were the voices in the local church of the 'whites-only' congregation singing, 'Praise the Lord'.

Standing alone outside was Tom, a black man, deeply spiritual, listening to the Sunday service in full swing. Jesus was passing by and began to talk to him.

'Tom,' he said, 'why have you not gone into the service?'

Tom said, 'I have tried but I am unable to get admission.'

Jesus smiled, clasped Tom by the shoulder and said, 'Don't worry, I know exactly how you feel. I've been trying to get into that church for years.'

SO YOU THINK YOU'VE GOT IT ...

The right of passage should tell you whether the club you want to join is worth the effort. Often it's not what you are but who you are that's important. It is sometimes not enough to believe and to sing off the same hymn sheet, but you have to look the part as well.

You need to consider, not only what you are going

to gain from joining any club, but what you will have to give up before you become an acceptable member.

> **GET THIS:**
> THE GOLDEN RULE IS: THOSE WHO HAVE
> THE GOLD MAKE THE RULES

39 *Da's Super Vision*

Michael's father knocks on his door at 7.30 in the morning. 'Get up, it's time to go to school,' he calls out.

Michael replies, 'Dad I don't want to go to school today.'

'Why not?' asks Michael's father.

'I will give you three good reasons,' says Michael. 'First, the weather is dreadful. Second, the kids tease me. Third, the teachers don't like me.'

'Ok, ok,' says the father. 'Now, Michael, I will give you three better reasons why you must go to school. First, it is your duty. Second, you are forty years old. Third, you are the headmaster!'

Life is difficult and some mornings it's hard just to get out of the bed, especially if you are the headmaster. Remember it's not easy to motivate others if you cannot motivate yourself. People have more need for good models than for critics. Most people don't leave organisations because they are dissatisfied with the organisation, but because they are dissatisfied with their manager. So even though you are the manager and feeling totally exhausted, throw your legs out of the bed – your heart and mind will soon follow and so will your staff.

GET THIS:
EXCUSES ARE NOT REASONS

40 *Designer Labels*

Tom, a humble man with low self-esteem, struggled through life thinking the best of others and only the worst of himself. On their first safari holiday he hacked his way through the jungle with Michael, his travelling companion. He burst out into an opening on marshy ground and, to his surprise, about fifty feet into the marsh was a crocodile, smug and contented with a man's head sticking out of its mouth. Tom, amazed, shouted at Michael, who was still making his way into the clearing: 'Hurry, Hurry, Michael! Look, have you ever seen the likes of that?'

'God, fellows like that give me a pain in the arse. What a poser, lying out there fast asleep in his Lacoste sleeping bag,' commented Michael.

SO YOU THINK YOU'VE GOT IT ...

Most people struggle through life while others make it look easy. If you are a loser, everybody else, no matter how difficult their circumstances, looks like a winner. Even when you are a winner there are hard times ahead where you may fail or struggle and it is then you will realise who your real friends are. However, if you are simply a poser and you spend your time chasing designer labels don't expect too much sympathy.

GET THIS:
IT IS HARD TO HAVE SYMPATHY FOR A POSER

41 *Striking Oil*

The rabbi died and went to Heaven but he found to his surprise that the Lord was not altogether pleased with him. He said to the Lord, 'what do you want of me, I led a good life on earth. I visited the synagogue everyday and prayed fervently to be more like Moses.'

'That,' said the Lord, 'is what bothered me, I would have been far happier if you had prayed to be more like yourself.'

SO YOU THINK YOU'VE GOT IT ...

The inner journey towards being ourselves is a much more arduous task than the outer journey of being like somebody else, no matter how exemplary or attractive they may seem. Golda Meir, a former Israeli prime minister, said of Moses, 'He took us through the desert for forty years in order to bring us to the one spot in the Middle East that has no oil!' Concentrate on being yourself. Self-awareness is an inner journey and all possibilities open up when that journey is undertaken. Sometimes the beginning of that inner journey requires a kick-start from outside, even from God Himself, but you might be lucky enough to strike oil at the end of the day.

GET THIS:
IT IS TEMPTING TO TRY TO IMITATE SOME-
ONE ELSE RATHER THAN BE YOURSELF

42 As Luck Would Have it

The adoring parents gave in to their children's pleading and got them a dog for Christmas. The dog was unanimously named Lucky by the children. On Stephen's Day he was petted and stroked, walked and fed. The next day he was petted and stroked but with half a walk and half fed. He was grudgingly fed and not walked at all the following day. On day four when he wasn't petted or stroked, walked or fed, the parents gave up in frustration and took over. In spite of the children's freshly made New Year's Resolutions to take really good care of their pet, the four-day pattern was repeated. Six months later, so they could get a weekend away, a little time for themselves and a well-earned rest, the parents decided to get a new home for Lucky and a new life for themselves. All hell broke loose, and the family was torn apart. Meanwhile Lucky, happy and carefree, adjusted to the new surroundings.

SO YOU THINK YOU'VE GOT IT ...

Those who are attached are not necessarily committed and those who are committed are not necessarily attached. Exit packages are designed primarily in the company's interest and with a view to whom they wish to retain. However, when downsizing takes place, it is frequently the committed who leave and the attached who stay. The dilemma is, the committed have upskilled themselves, have confidence in their own ability and are more likely to take the risk of leaving and going elsewhere. They have mastered the art of being passionate about their work and are somewhat dispassionate about the company. The attached may or may not have the necessary transferable skills but they have emotionally married themselves to the company and are reluctant to leave even when it's in their best interest. Lucky was smart enough to attach himself to the committed.

> GET THIS:
> ## ATTACHMENT AND COMMITMENT SHOULD NOT BE CONFUSED

Chapter 6
Maestro or Madness

Lester Piggott, who was deaf in one ear, normally gave a £1 tip to the stable lad in charge of the previous day's winner he had ridden from Henry Cecil's stable. One day he had to be reminded by an old groom about the pound he owed him for the previous day's winner. Lester frowned and asked, 'what did you say?'

'What about the pound for yesterday?' the groom repeated.

Lester replied, 'That's my deaf ear, go round to my good ear.'

'What about a couple of pounds for yesterday?' the old stager repeated.

Lester mumbled, 'Would you ever go back to my one pound ear.'

SO YOU THINK YOU'VE GOT IT ...

Suggesting change is one thing, getting it is another and keeping it in place is a third. Stabilising the new order is an essential part of any change process and it only comes after the initial changes have been accepted. Senator Mitchell, of the United States, commenting on the negotiations in Northern Ireland said, 'people have to realise that having a peace agreement in place is not the same thing as making a peace agreement work.' The stabilisation process is about agreeing and institutionalising the changes, it is about replacing the old order with a new order and making the new policies, procedures and reward systems the new status quo. It is about embedding the new culture in the organisation. If you are not speedy, fleet-footed and diligent about doing this, people will quickly revert to the old order.

> GET THIS:
> IF PEOPLE DON'T LIKE WHAT YOU ARE
> PROPOSING THEY WILL GIVE YOU
> THE DEAF EAR

44 *Nell*

Cavan is a proud Ulster county on the republican side of the Irish border. Its inhabitants like nothing more than to be underestimated, many things go unstated, tradition dies hard and living memory is only the beginning of the story.

Cavan is the last county in Ireland where funeral offerings to the priest died a death. Their removal was considered a clerical error by the hierarchy but it was a mighty relief to the local community who often missed the final farewell to friend and neighbour rather than face the indignity of having their small contribution acknowledged from the altar to a full congregation by an austere parish priest. Humiliation all round!

One of the finer traditions to survive was the invitation to members of the congregation to speak well of the dead before the removal of their remains from the church. It was always regarded as right and proper to finish on an upbeat note, for it is said of the Irish, 'All our wars are happy and all our songs are sad.'

It was hard to know whether the death of Joe Brady was a sad or a happy occasion. He was known locally as the last of the small spenders. He was economical with everything, including the truth. Never a man to use two words when one would do, he was slow to pass a compliment, quick to complain and double-quick to grasp an opportunity, even at the expense of his neighbour. Despised within the community, he was still one of their own.

When the funeral mass concluded, the celebrant, in the time honoured way, called for somebody in the congregation to speak the *cúpla focail* on behalf of the deceased. His invitation was met with silence, coughing and clearing of the throats, and then nothing, not a stir in the church. The parish priest, somewhat taken aback, once again intervened and pleaded for someone to do the decent thing. The tension was palpable. To the surprise of everyone, Nell, a professional mourner, known rather astutely as Death Nell, as she was never heard to utter a kind word about anybody, stood up and announced piously, 'However bad Joe Brady was, he wasn't half as bad as his brother!'

SO YOU THINK YOU'VE GOT IT ...

Silence doesn't always mean approval; it often means dissent. 'It is not the noise of my enemies that worries me, it is the silence of my friends,' said Oscar Wilde. People rarely speak up and put their heads on the block, thinking it better to keep their heads down and their mouths shut, for silence may be misinterpreted but it can never be misquoted.

GET THIS:
IF OFFENCE IS IN THE OFFING,
THE LESS SAID THE BETTER

Mikhail Gorbachev was asked what drove him and gave him the courage to dismantle Communism in the Soviet Union. He replied that he got his inspiration from a Polish shipyard worker, Lech Walesa, who helped overthrow the Communist regime in Poland.

Lech Walesa was asked from whom he got his inspiration and he said, 'From a black leader named Nelson Mandela, who challenged apartheid in South Africa from a prison cell against impossible odds.'

Nelson Mandela, on being asked the same question, said he took his lead from the great civil rights activist, Martin Luther King, of the United States.

Luther King, in reply to the question, said he got his courage and inspiration from a black woman, Rosa Parks, who refused to go to the back of a bus in Alabama.

Rosa Parks, on being asked what idealism inspired her, said, 'None, I was just tired and frustrated and thought "enough is enough, I'm not going to the back of the bus".'

SO YOU THINK YOU'VE GOT IT ...

Tired and frustrated is often the place from where real change begins. The seedbed for change is often dissatisfaction with the status quo which can be fed by a vision of a better future. For every ninety-nine historians in an organisation there is probably only one prophet with a dream to share. This dream may be seen by others as either a challenge or a threat; what seems a small step for the visionary may seem an impossible and negotiable step for others. As a result the visionary voice can be intimidated or drowned out by the many voices as the status quo regroups and draws the wagons around in a circle. In those circumstances, the visionary voice needs to hold steady, take the bold step and cry 'enough is enough'.

GET THIS:
BEING BOLD FOR SOME IS TAKING THEIR SEAT IN THE SENATE; FOR OTHERS IT IS TAKING THEIR SEAT ON THE BUS

46 *The Piano Player*

Many years ago, I brought my wife out on one of our wedding anniversary nights. I was totally unprepared but showed the utmost confidence.

She had expressed an interest in dining in a specific restaurant in the Dublin dockland area. I went to the door and asked for a table for two. A gentleman in a black dinner jacket, bow tie and with a friendly demeanour said, 'We have no table. We are fully booked up as far as I know, but I'm only the piano player.'

I pleaded with him and shared my plight. He conceded and let me sit at reception while he checked out the situation.

He came back five minutes later and said, 'Mr O'Donnell, I'm very sorry, we are fully booked out, there is no table and there is nothing I can do. As I said, I'm only the piano player.'

SO YOU THINK YOU'VE GOT IT ...

If you are explaining or complaining, you are losing. It is important to separate out influencing from emotional discharging, making something happen, as distinct from getting heard.

Picking the right people who are in a position to influence things is a necessary first step. It's amazing the number of people who seek advice on crucial issues from those who are not in charge of their own lives. Picking someone who knows the problem, who cares, and can do something about it, is the important starting point of influencing and it is only the beginning.

> GET THIS:
> IF YOU ARE REDUCED TO PLEADING,
> PLEAD WITH SOMEONE WHO HAS THE
> POWER TO SOLVE THE PROBLEM

47 An Academic Lion

Leo the Lion, missing from Dublin Zoo for two weeks, was asked how he was found. Leo answered, 'For thirteen days I went to the university and ate a professor and on the fourteenth day I was foolish enough to eat the tea lady!'

Who is and who is not important to an organisation is often a matter of conjecture and is not always reflected by their position on the organisation chart. The lion's share of the essential work in an organisation is mundane, routine and done at the back of the shop by unsung heroes who get little if any acknowledgement from organisations. Their significance is not recognised until they leave or suffer burnout at the hands of the organisation. The front of house glamorous jobs and indeed the business couldn't survive without their contribution.

GET THIS:
IT'S PEOPLE'S CONTRIBUTION, NOT THEIR STATUS, THAT ADDS VALUE

48 Frank O'Neill

In Dalymount Park many years ago, Shamrock Rovers were playing in a European Championship game. A player named Frank O'Neill played for them at outside right. 'Twinkling Feet' Frank O'Neill was smallish, fast and nimble, and was very proud of his dribbling skills. There was nothing he liked to do more than beat a man with the ball, not once but twice or even more if the opportunity presented itself.

Twenty minutes into the game Frank picked up the ball on the halfway line and ghosted past the first tackle. 'Go on, O'Neill,' shouted a man excitedly beside me on the terrace. Frank slipped the ball through the legs of the next defender. 'You're a genius, O'Neill,' cried the voice from the terrace. He rounded the third defender. 'Keep going,' roared the voice. He showed the ball to the fourth defender and glided past him. 'That's my boy, O'Neill,' exclaimed the man on the terrace. Frank got to the edge of the box and shot, the ball slid off the outside of his boot and hit the corner flag. 'Jaysus, O'Neill, you are only a ham,' shouted the now angry and frustrated fan.

When all the excitement had died down a voice from behind the disconsolate supporter boomed, 'He's not a ham, a ham can be cured.'

48 *Frank O'Neill*

There are two types of people in the world: those who finish what they start and everyone else. When you don't finish the job the good work is quickly forgotten. Finish what you set out to do, otherwise somebody will get you – more often than not it will be a spectator, a person who couldn't even attempt what you set out to do in the first place.

> GET THIS:
> THERE IS NOTHING AS IRRELEVANT IN
> SPORT OR IN LIFE AS THE HALF-TIME SCORE

49 Baby it's Cold Outside

It was 7 a.m. in the high support hospital ward; the day shift would be coming on in an hour. Nurse Dowling was completing the reports and paperwork at the nurse's station in anticipation of the change over to the new shift.

The phone rang, she lifted it and said, 'Nurse Dowling speaking, may I help you?'

'Yes, I hope so,' answered the soft-spoken south Galway accent. 'Kevin Considine was admitted to the hospital on Monday week last with chest pains and dizzy spells. I believe he is now in St Joseph's Ward and I am just wondering how he is?' enquired the courteous caller.

'Very satisfactory,' replied Nurse Dowling. 'Kevin was moved here from coronary care on Tuesday morning. The procedure seems to have gone well and all his vital signs are good.' She continued, 'His heartbeat was regularised and his blood pressure has improved and is all but under control.'

'Good, good,' interjected the concerned voice.

'He was pretty agitated the first couple of days but that goes with the condition,' assured Nurse Dowling.

'Is there anything else?' enquired the obviously now relieved caller.

'Well, we are awaiting the results of a scan but the consultant, Mr Murphy, is optimistic it should now be clear.'

'Good, good,' added the gentleman again.

'Kevin had a very restful night and I don't think you

should be worrying,' Nurse Dowling comforted him. 'He will be glad to hear you called, who will I say called?'

'It's ok,' the man replied at the other end of the phone. 'I am Kevin Considine. I have been in that bed for over a week and I couldn't find out a damn thing about my condition.'

> SO YOU THINK YOU'VE GOT IT ...

In every walk of life there are insiders and outsiders. Our lives are permeated by these roles. As insiders we have the information and not necessarily the perspective, and as outsiders the perspective and not necessarily the information. People tend to be unduly precious about information and feed it to outsiders in dribs and drabs or on a need-to-know basis. The possession of information is a powerful statement and the use to which it is put says an awful lot about the insider. The outsider, through frustration, is driven to use many creative ways of getting information to piece together the full picture. The ultimate step may be to become an insider to gain the power you need to succeed.

> GET THIS:
> INFORMATION IS POWER

50 The Church Mouse

The parish priest, Father Murphy, giving his Sunday sermon, told the parishioners that the clergy had been demented all week by a mouse on the loose in the church. They nicknamed her Mona Lisa, as she would just smile at them and then somehow vanish. With great difficulty they tracked her down. She had made her home in the collection box at the back of the church!

On being asked by her captor, the priest, why she had chosen the collection box for her home, she meekly replied, 'sure nobody ever goes near it.'

Father Murphy, after a suitable pause announced, 'We will now take up the collection.'

SO YOU THINK YOU'VE GOT IT ...

A good story is particularly useful, especially when sensitive issues have to be addressed. Talking about money is one of those issues; you will always be busy if you are working for nothing, but eventually you have to put a price on your work and ask for it. Some people don't like asking for money but everybody hates parting with it. In circumstances like these a good story is a great companion and may loosen people's grip on their wallets.

GET THIS:
THERE IS GREAT SAFETY IN A GOOD STORY

Chapter 7
Sense or Nonsense

51 Common Sense

Out walking one afternoon, young John asked his father, 'how does the electricity go through the wires between the poles?'

'Could never figure that out,' said the Da, 'could never figure out electricity!'

'Da, how is the rain made?' asked John looking at the clouds in the sky.

'I never really fully understood that myself,' replied the Da, 'never really understood that.'

'Da, how do birds fly?'

'Well now, that is a real mystery,' answered the father, 'a real mystery.'

Several miles and many questions later young John said politely, 'I hope you don't mind me asking all these questions, Da?'

'Not at all,' said the father, 'not at all,' patting John on the head. 'How else are you going to learn my son, how else are you going to learn?'

SO YOU THINK YOU'VE GOT IT ...

Curiosity is a wonderful teacher but it needs encouragement. Young males, above all, are looking for support and a strong role model. Ignorance is not an endearing characteristic to model; it doesn't shed much light and is unlikely to win you any fans. Questions are very important, but the answers need to reflect that they have been heard.

51 *Common Sense*

As a youngster at the racecourse my father stopped me when I was interrupting a conversation between the legendary racehorse trainer, Paddy Prendergast, and himself, and counselled, 'Shish Eamon, keep quiet, you will never learn while you are talking.'

When you stop talking and start to listen, have you any idea what you are listening for? Sometimes it is what is half said, or not said at all, that is important; interpreting nuances correctly is essential to a full understanding of the information you are getting, especially when there is money to be made!

GET THIS:
WISDOM LISTENS, KNOWLEDGE TALKS

Ivan, living in Russia, met his neighbour Mikhail in the local village. Ivan conveyed the news: 'My son, Boris, ran away from home two days ago.'

'That's bad!' said Mikhail.

'No,' said Ivan. 'That's good. He arrived home with a herd of wild horses yesterday.'

'That's good!' said Mikhail.

'No, that's bad,' said Ivan. 'He fell off one of the horses and broke his leg.'

'That's bad!' said Mikhail.

'No, that's good,' said Ivan. 'Last night the army called to the house to conscript him, but they did not take him.'

'That's good!' said Mikhail.

'No, that's bad,' said Ivan. 'For now we cannot afford provisions for the winter.'

SO YOU THINK YOU'VE GOT IT ...

Things are rarely simple, conclusive, good or bad, right or wrong, they are just interesting. The more things unfold the more complex they become so there is no sense in jumping to early conclusions. It helps if you listen to the full story. Judgement should be made only after the data is gathered; to do so beforehand is to pre-judge, and that is called prejudice.

GET THIS:
COMPLEXITY HAS A GREAT FUTURE, WHAT WITH ONE THING ALWAYS LEADING TO ANOTHER

53 *The Vernacular*

The contemplative order, in which monks rarely spoke, was celebrating Brother Patrick's tenth anniversary at which he was invited to comment briefly on his experience to date: 'The food is absolutely dreadful and has been for some time,' he observed.

'Very well and thank you,' said the saintly prior with some sympathy.

On being invited to speak on his twentieth anniversary Patrick commented: 'The bed is rock hard and needs to be replaced.'

'Very well, thank you,' said the prior, shaking his head.

On the occasion of his thirtieth anniversary he stated definitively: 'I am leaving.'

'I thought as much Patrick,' commented the now frustrated prior. 'You are so negative, all you have done since you joined us is complain, complain, complain.'

SO YOU THINK YOU'VE GOT IT ...

When you invite people into a conversation you should listen to what they have to say. More often than not there will be a difference of opinion but you may get a clue as to their thoughts and intended actions. Exit interviews are particularly important, as the person leaving has nothing to lose while you have everything to gain.

GET THIS:
HONEST CRITICISM IS HARD TO TAKE

54 *Accidents Rarely Happen*

John, on being interviewed for the job of pointsman by Iarnród Éireann, was faced with a fairly intimidating panel.

One of the sterner faced gentlemen took a deep breath, stroked his grey hair, leaned forward and with some authority popped the following question: 'The Cork to Dublin train has just left Limerick Junction, there is a runaway train on the line from Thurles, the two trains are heading for a crash. What would you do?'

'Well,' said John, 'I would run up the track, grab a flare and fire it into the air to warn the oncoming trains.'

The interviewer leaned back, took off his glasses, tapped them on the side of the desk and said, 'There are no flares.'

'Well,' said John, 'I would run up the track, grab a flag and stand between the lines and wave it at the oncoming trains.'

The interviewer with a breaking smile replied, 'There are no flares, there is no flag, what would you do?'

Thinking hard, John replied, 'I would run up the track, take off my jacket, stand between the lines, jump up and down and wave it frantically at the oncoming trains.'

The interviewer confidently stated, 'There are no flares, there is no flag and you have no jacket, what would you do?'

John immediately replied, 'I would run the 300

metres home, grab my Uncle Pat and sit him on the bridge.'

'Why would you do that?' asked the interviewer incredulously!

'Because my Uncle Pat has never seen a head-on crash,' said John.

Hypothetical questions are frequently used as the cornerstone of selection interviews but their value is doubtful. They explore and test for creativity and verbal fluency but not knowledge and may be put to best use in recruiting for hypothetical jobs. They are often the reason why so many highly articulate, but incompetent people are hired. In the real world these questions are often a cover-up for lack of preparation and are more a reflection on the incompetence of the interviewer rather than the competence of the interviewee.

> GET THIS:
> HYPOTHETICAL QUESTIONS DESERVE
> NOTHING BETTER THAN
> HYPOTHETICAL ANSWERS

The mother, dragging her son Harry away from a premiership match on TV said, 'Hurry up, run down to the shops and get me some bread, butter, sugar and tea, some potatoes and peas. If you forget anything, forget the peas.'

Five minutes later Harry arrived back from the shops puffing and panting and asked, 'Ma, apart from the peas, what else did you want?'

SO YOU THINK YOU'VE GOT IT ...

Hurry sickness is different to busy sickness. When people get excited speed becomes the dominant driver of behaviour. There is an old saying, 'if you want something done give it to a busy person'. If you are busy, rushed or fussed draw up a list and prioritise it, be specific about the deadline, emphasise what you want, not what you don't want. 'Hurry up' is not good enough, especially if the listener is preoccupied with something else and anxious to get back to it.

GET THIS:
SPEED AND PROGRESS ARE NOT NECESSARILY THE SAME THING

56 *The Beijing Robber*

A man in Beijing appeared before the judge accused of snatching a bag of money from a security van in broad daylight. He grabbed the bag and started running through the crowded streets pursued by several amazed security guards before being caught.

Asked by the judge how he thought he would get away with it, he said, 'I didn't think anybody would notice.'

SO YOU THINK YOU'VE GOT IT ...

You often see people in organisations being mugged by highly intelligent colleagues, thinking nobody will notice, yet when called to account for their behaviour they defend themselves by quoting company policy. Company policy usually means there is no understandable reason for what you have just witnessed. To get away with dark behaviour in an organisation, a culture of fear inevitably has to exist. The survival of this culture depends upon disguise. So the challenge is: can we face the fear and unmask that disguise? Only when this question is addressed will people sit up and take notice.

GET THIS:
WHEN MOST PEOPLE DON'T KNOW WHAT TO DO, THEY GO INTO DENIAL

57 *Death's Grip*

In India there is a unique breed of monkey considered by the natives to be something of a delicacy.

The natives have developed a very creative way of catching their agile foe. They get a coconut, top it and quarter fill the coconut with rice. The mixture of rice and coconut milk gives off an irresistible aroma which attracts the monkeys into the clearing where the coconuts have been left. The monkeys put their fists into the coconut, grab a fistful of rice and then cannot get their bulging fist back out of the narrow opening. The natives casually walk over to them, knowing they will refuse to let go of the rice, decapitate them, and fry the monkey's brains as a delicacy.

SO YOU THINK YOU'VE GOT IT ...

One of the primary causes of failure is often self-inflicted: it is the inability of people and organisations to let go. Sometimes you have to stand down your own preferences to allow for creativity and the emergence of a positive new future – often easier said than done. If you cannot let go of opinions, issues and the past, there is always someone standing by anxious and willing to fry your brains.

GET THIS:
TO HAVE ANY FUTURE YOU HAVE TO LET GO

58 *Visiting the Dark Side*

It was a dark November night, the clouds obliterated the sky, the moon and the stars. I was visiting my mother in North County Dublin and with dipped lights I pulled into the semicircular driveway. The porch area was lit by a subtle yellow light which threw out a glow rather than a beam. I noticed my young nephew peering around the outer perimeter of the lighted area, apparently looking for something. 'What's up?' I asked.

'My Da has lost his car keys,' he said.

'Hold on and I will pull back, put the head beams on and give you more light.'

Both of us searched for five or ten minutes and eventually, out of frustration I asked, 'Where did he lose them?'

'Well, we were playing football earlier and he thinks he lost them over beside the ditch!'

'Why aren't you looking over there then?' I asked impatiently.

'Because I'm afraid of the dark,' he replied.

SO YOU THINK YOU'VE GOT IT ...

All of us are afraid of the dark. When we shake our family tree there is one thing for sure – a monkey is bound to fall off. We don't know what skeleton is in the cupboard and we don't know what the dark side of our nature will reveal. If we knew everything in life there would be no mystery or magic. Discovery is an open-ended process but it often requires shining a light into life's darker corners.

> GET THIS:
> SOME ANSWERS ARE IN LIFE'S
> DARKER CORNERS

59 *Bill Shankley*

In the late seventies, Ireland played Argentina in soccer in Lansdowne Road. Maradona, then seventeen years old, came on in the second half for Argentina and showed flashes of the brilliance that later marked his career. Ireland played well in spots during the first half but 'didn't see as much of the ball as they would have liked'. Ireland's player manager, John Giles', half-time talk reportedly went as follows. Bending down he picked up a ball: 'This is a ball, when the opposition have it they can score, when we have it we can score and they can't score. We haven't enough of the ball, now let's go out and get the fecking ball.'

The focus on the primary task should never be lost. To quote Bill Shankley, the legendary Liverpool manager, 'Football is more important than life'. John Giles says, 'Football is about results'. Eamon Dunphy calls football, 'the beautiful game'. Is it a beautiful game, is it about results or something more? Shankley told his players, 'If you find yourself in the penalty area and you don't know what to do, stick the ball in the back of the net and we will discuss your options later.' Now that's focus.

GET THIS:
THE MAIN THING IS TO KEEP THE MAIN THING THE MAIN THING

Chapter 8

Rethink Everything

60 *A Small Irish or a Double*

It was a beautiful May day on Lough Conn in County Mayo. The fisherman and the gilly were relaxed and content in one another's company. Their thoughts were turning from fishing to their packed lunch and light refreshments, when the fisherman caught a glimpse of the slightest of movements at the side of the boat.

He looked down and saw a most unusual sight. To his amazement there was a large eel with its head bobbing above the water with a frog in its mouth. Instinctively he grabbed the eel, took the frog from its mouth and threw the frog into the safety of the boat. Feeling sorry for having deprived the eel of its breakfast, he reached into his bag, took out a flask of whiskey, unscrewed the cap and poured several drops of Jameson down the eel's throat. He then placed the eel back in the lake.

He sat back in the boat feeling quite chuffed with himself and thought, 'I've sorted that out and I am truly happy, the frog is happy, the eel is happy, in fact everybody is happy.' He and the gilly began to lunch, relax and share a sandwich.

Minutes later there was a rat-tat-tat on the side of the boat. The fisherman bent over and, to his utter astonishment, there was the eel, this time with two frogs in its mouth.

60 *A Small Irish or a Double*

Consciously or unconsciously we create the environment that encourages the behaviour we get. We are hoping for one behaviour, while more often rewarding the opposite. In business we invariably overload the willing staff with work and, through a sense of self-preservation, provide the unwilling or difficult staff with insufficient work. As a result the willing are punished, the unwilling are rewarded and, furthermore, they are left with idle time on their hands to create mischief.

> GET THIS:
> THE BEHAVIOUR YOU REWARD IS THE
> BEHAVIOUR YOU GET

Mother loved lamb. She had a bounce in her step on lamb Sundays. When my wife and I were first married and had moved into our own home, we went through all the rituals and observed all the protocols expected of us. When we were well practised in the art of cooking, we casually invited my mother and father to Sunday lunch.

'Mother, would you like to come to lunch on Sunday and we'll have your favourite, a roast leg of lamb?'

Mother immediately replied, 'Eamon, you know I would love to but not this Sunday. I will come over as soon as things get back to normal!'

We have had many roast legs of lamb since but sadly things have not yet got back to normal.

SO YOU THINK YOU'VE GOT IT ...

We are living, if not in a time of constant crises, then in a time of constant change. However, normality is supposedly the rule and abnormality the exception. When did you last have a normal day in the home, the school or the office?

Learn to accept constant change and to embrace the abnormal. A shift of mindset is required to avoid change fatigue and that shift is to view normality as the exception and abnormality as the rule.

Intelligence has been defined as the ability to hold two opposing ideas in your mind at the same time and still function. If you can manage that, your day will become a lot more predictable and life a lot less stressful.

> ### GET THIS:
> ## IF YOU ACCEPT ABNORMALITY AS THE RULE YOU WILL LEARN TO DEVOUR PROBLEMS

Peter's strength on the farm was machinery and machine maintenance. I felt he was particularly good at it because of the amount of practice he got! On one occasion when I was complaining about the amount of machine breakdowns at vital times, he commented, 'machinery will never break down in the shed, only when it's being used.' My father agreed, but used to get quite frustrated with Peter's inability to take his own advice and not put the machinery at unnecessary risk during the harvest. Every harvest Peter invariably started cutting the corn at the outer edges of the field; it somehow looked neater, he felt. The problem was the combine-harvester swallowed all the debris near the ditches and, as a result, often choked up and broke down. My father pleaded with him one day, as only he could: 'Peter, will you ever save the harvest first and then do the headland!'

SO YOU THINK YOU'VE GOT IT ...

There is some evidence to suggest that rats are brighter than people. Rats get tired of pressing the same coloured button without reward, they give up and sensibly move on to a different coloured one. People apparently never tire; they persist beyond reason, not only in pressing the same button, but additionally in banging their heads off the wall, kicking the furniture and finally tearing their hair out in frustration. If you do what you always did you will get what you always got. Move on. Don't spend eighty per cent of your time on the headland and outer edges of the field while watching the rest of the crop wasting away. It can be tempting, but you might just have a breakdown. Remember the old eighty/twenty rule: twenty per cent of your effort will yield you eighty per cent of the results. Put that in the bank first.

> GET THIS:
> DON'T BECOME OBSESSED WITH A
> SEDUCTIVE SIDESHOW AT THE EXPENSE
> OF YOUR MAIN TASK

63 *Diving for Cover*

Eamon Darcy, a renowned goalkeeper in the late sixties and early seventies with the Dublin soccer clubs, Drumcondra and Shamrock Rovers, was well known as something of a character. In O'Connell Street one day he was struck by a bus. Asked by a reporter what happened, he recalled, 'I was walking past Clery's and was crossing to the GPO on the other side of the street when a bus driver recognised me and nodded in my direction. I automatically dived. Unfortunately, I dived into the pathway of an oncoming bus.'

'What did you do that for?' the reporter enquired, shaking his head in disbelief.

Eamon answered, 'Habit. A lifetime of habit. When I was playing soccer if anybody nodded in my direction I automatically dived.'

SO YOU THINK YOU'VE GOT IT ...

Habits are ingrained and become a pattern and often a first response. Changing lifetime habits is difficult. For professional golfers, there is nothing more difficult than changing their grip. It's so difficult they refuse to call it change, they refer to it as adjusting their grip. So don't attempt to change lifetime habits, instead make adjustments as it is much easier to readjust later on. If you don't, you may well end up throwing yourself under a bus.

GET THIS:
ADAPTABILITY IS THE KEY TO SURVIVAL

64 The Unexpected

It was fair day in Killorglin, Co. Kerry, and Seamus brought his pride and joy to the fair: a five-year-old cow named Bell, the likes of which he never had before.

That evening his neighbour, Patsy Sullivan, known locally as *Súil Amháin* because he kept one eye on local affairs, happened to be leaning against the pillar of his gate, relaxed and smoking his pipe. He spotted Seamus returning home alone from the fair, slightly inebriated.

'What was trade like?' the shrewd Patsy enquired. 'Did you get a good price for Bell?'

'Well now, it was like this Patsy,' answered Seamus, 'I didn't get as much as I expected but then I didn't expect I would.' And he bade Patsy goodnight!

SO YOU THINK YOU'VE GOT IT ...

Managing your own and others' expectations is one of the great arts in life. Parents often experience disappointment because their children do not live up to their expectations. The opposite is also true: children get disappointed because their parents are not perfect. Unrealistic expectations set you up for failure. Be realistic and help people meet the standards on which you have both agreed.

GET THIS:
UNREALISTIC EXPECTATIONS CAUSE NOTHING BUT GRIEF

The rabbi, living in Moscow after the Second World War, visited the synagogue every day. He was met by the same soldier at arms outside the synagogue. Though he was very familiar with the rabbi, he clicked his heels and blocked the entrance to the synagogue with his rifle. He barked out, 'Who are you, and what are you doing here?'

'I am the rabbi and I am going to pray,' answered the rabbi consistently.

One day, on leaving the synagogue the rabbi, inspired, said to the soldier, 'When you leave the army, I will pay you 100 dinos a day to come here, to stop me every morning when I'm entering the synagogue and ask me, who am I and what am I doing here!'

SO YOU THINK YOU'VE GOT IT ...

In a world where activity is more highly regarded than achievement, and efficiency more highly regarded than effectiveness, somebody has to ask the tough questions. Friends are often too polite and it sometimes falls to those who appear hostile to us to inspire us and allow us to revisit the basics. Remember, a persistent or impertinent question is often the gateway to a pertinent answer.

GET THIS:
THE ROUTE OFTEN GETS LOST IN THE ROUTINE

Dessie, the Dubliner, and Con, from Cork, had been mates all their lives and had great regard for one another. From their early teens, both had worked on building sites in London and New York; Dessie to earn enough to fund his education and Con to earn some serious money. Con was very proud of his background. His father, a greyhound trainer, had taught him to break from the traps early and get noticed. Con, a believer in Brendan Behan's dictum, 'A Corkman with an inferiority complex thinks he's just as good as anybody else', carried himself with that authority. The lads were invariably called on when hard work was required and ideas were to be put into action.

The opening of the local festival was due and things were getting tight. The lads were asked to put up the massive nine-foot wide sign on the outskirts of the village. Unknown to them, the 'brainstrust' had erected the two upright poles twelve feet apart.

Dessie and Con lifted the sign and Dessie, trying to adjust it, shouted to Con, 'I'm about three feet short at this end.'

Con replied, 'It's perfect at my end!'

SO YOU THINK YOU'VE GOT IT ...

Confidence and self-assurance are wonderful attributes, however, they should not impair your judgement. If everyone does their 'own thing' to the exclusion of all else, that's exactly what gets done – everyone's own thing – and the primary task is rarely accomplished. The very notion of organised work gives rise to two opposing requirements: the division of labour into various tasks to be performed and the co-ordination of these tasks to accomplish the overall goal. Personal satisfaction from achieving individual targets should not come at the expense of the organisation's goals.

GET THIS:
INDIVIDUAL AND ORGANISATIONAL
GOALS ARE OFTEN POLES APART

67 *Joe Montana*

Joe Montana was a famous quarterback for the San Francisco 49ers. In one of the early games in his career, he called a time-out and pleaded with his defence to give him more protection and cover. He lectured them on how the opposing team was getting too many tackles and how he couldn't get the ball to his runners. 'Go to it,' he said, 'and remember, more protection.'

When the next play took place, his defence stayed static. The opposing team came down on Joe like a ton of bricks and he was buried under a mass of bodies.

Bruised and battered, he struggled to his feet and his team-mates came to him. 'Now Joe,' they said. 'That's what it's like when we are not protecting you.'

SO YOU THINK YOU'VE GOT IT ...

Being protected doesn't mean you are immune from the ordinary trials of the world. We sometimes expect too much from our champions and need to get things into perspective. We may have too high an expectation of the protection we can be afforded from the top or little understanding of the natural hostility to the work we do within the organisation. A champion should only be called upon to help sort out the big issues. The rest we should tidy up ourselves.

GET THIS:
YOUR CHAMPION IN THE ORGANISATION CAN ONLY DO SO MUCH

Chapter 9
Ego Ergo Ugo

The local parish priest, who preferred to be addressed by his proper title of 'Canon', was educated, sophisticated and sure of his place on earth and in Heaven. He was noted over the years as a talented preacher; his sermons always had meaning and relevance for his congregation. Of late however there was some grumbling in the parish about the extraordinary and extending length of his sermons. Sensitive to the needs of his flock and aware of his public image, he asked the altar boy to take note of his sermon at the eleven o'clock mass that Sunday.

After mass he bid good day to the parishioners on the steps of the church. He made his way back to the sacristy and addressed the young altar boy. 'Well my good man, did you think the sermon was too long?'

'No,' replied the altar boy sheepishly, 'not at the beginning, Canon.'

SO YOU THINK YOU'VE GOT IT ...

The golden rule of effective feedback is to focus on what the recipient has the capacity and motivation to change. There is only so much you can say that is helpful. Everything else is an over production and tends to meet the anxiety needs of the giver, not the developmental needs of the receiver and ultimately it diminishes both the giver and the receiver. The vulnerable one in a feedback situation is often the provider of the feedback. Those in

68 *Collateral Damage*

the lower echelons of the organisations, even with encouragement, are slow to give feedback for obvious reasons. They might get hit by a cannon!

> GET THIS:
> COMMUNICATION HAPPENS NATURALLY
> WHEN YOU MAKE THINGS SAFE

Jack Diffney lived alone with his two nearly teenage boys, Jimmy and Joseph. They were good kids, friendly, vibrant, hardworking and bright, however they had one failing: they used bad language, even in front of their father. Sick and tired of the bad language, Jack warned the children he would put an end to it and if he heard another word of foul language out of their mouths there would be a price to be paid. The following day he asked the eldest boy, Jimmy, what would he like for breakfast.

'I'll have a fecking fried egg,' Jimmy casually replied.

All hell broke loose and, true to his word, Jack took action and gave Jimmy a good clip on the ear that sent him flying halfway across the room. He then turned to his youngest son, Joseph, and enquired, 'Now, what will you have for breakfast?'

Turning to him in horror Joseph exclaimed, 'Da, the one thing I don't want is a fecking fried egg!'

SO YOU THINK YOU'VE GOT IT ...

Temperament plays a huge part in managing people and it influences whether you engender love, respect or fear. In today's macho world it seems perfectly acceptable to manage through respect, with a hint of fear, and apparently even more acceptable to manage through fear with little hint of respect. However, we are long past the galley ship era when forty good lashes got the desired response. Wouldn't it be nice if people rallied to the cause just because they liked you and you were a worthy role model? My father used to say, 'example is the best teacher'. There are too few worthy role models for young males today and a clip on the ear won't improve that situation.

> GET THIS:
> SOME EXPERIENCE ONLY THE TEMPER
> AND NOT THE TEACHING

Jack, the lodger, left the house for work having asked the landlady to cook his favourite breakfast of baked beans. He was very hungry and ate seven cans of beans that particular morning.

The guards called around to the house later that day and showed the landlady a photograph of a man who had thrown himself off the Halfpenny Bridge into the Liffey and drowned.

'Is that your lodger?' they asked.

'Yes,' she replied, rather shocked, 'and I don't understand it because when Jack left here this morning he was full of beans!'

Good decisions are a mixture of our emotional insight and our intellectual analysis. Don't be impetuous. Never act on your first thoughts unless they are your final thoughts on the matter as well. We often get caught up in an adrenalin rush. Trust your gut, but first run your emotions past your brain to be sure to be sure.

GET THIS:
LIFE OR DEATH DECISIONS SHOULD NOT
BE MADE WHEN YOU ARE EITHER FULL OF
BEANS OR TOTALLY DEPRESSED

71 *Water Pressure or Blood Pressure?*

Cecil was on the bike cycling to his work in Dublin's Financial Services Centre. It was a July day, he was up early, had recorded the dawn chorus and checked his emails, had his tea, toast and glass of orange juice, and donned his safety helmet for the pleasant cycle in by the coast road from Dun Laoghaire. Better, he thought, than the hard-topped hat and the crowded tubes in London which he had just left to come to his native city and real tranquillity.

He passed what used to be Boland's Mills and the new Grand Canal Street Station – signs of the Celtic Tiger and real progress, he contentedly thought. Meanwhile, the firemen in Tara Street Station were doing their regular training drill at 8.30 a.m. They were particularly anxious to win the Best Station in Ireland award in which they had been runners up for the past three years. However, a drought in Dublin over the past two months had resulted in inconsistent water pressure and presented a unique problem to be overcome.

It was 8.37 a.m. as Cecil passed the fire station; it was 8.37 a.m. when the water pressure suddenly increased and blasted down the hose. Finbar, the fireman, panicked, lost control and spun with the out of control hose. Cecil, the cyclist, was knocked to the ground with the full force of the water, washed over to the wall at Trinity College with the second swivel and got an unsolicited encore with the third when he stood up.

71 *Water Pressure or Blood Pressure?*

Finbar finally got the hose under control but Cecil singularly failed that test with his temper. He stood up, threw his battered helmet to the ground and shouted at the apologetic fireman, 'You wouldn't do that to me if I was on fire.'

SO YOU THINK YOU'VE GOT IT ...

At a University College Dublin society meeting, a student asked Seán Lemass, the taoiseach at the time, 'What is the most important attribute for a young budding politician?'

'The ability not to take offence,' he replied. 'If you get up in the morning and just stand outside your front door you will probably offend the milkman. Can you imagine what it's like when you try to do something?'

GET THIS:
THE SECRET OF SUCCESS IS NOT TO
TAKE LIFE PERSONALLY

I was at an IMI/Enterprise Ireland dinner as a counsellor for participants who were attending a programme on transformation. As I walked through the bar area, I glanced at the TV and saw 'Blackburn 1, Manchester United 0'. I sat down at the table and casually remarked, 'The latest score in the big game is Blackburn 1, Man. United 0.'

One participant punched the air and said, 'Great!', another said 'Damn!' and a third said, 'I don't care, I'm an Arsenal supporter.' I said, 'I'm Eamon. I'm a counsellor on the programme. I just give data; I don't express an opinion.'

> SO YOU THINK YOU'VE GOT IT ...

One of the things I discovered when teaching in the IMI was that every opinion you express can be contentious and that the simplest data gets judged. I experienced three types of students: those who wanted to focus on something very specific; those who were open to anything; and those who had little or no interest in learning. One group had the ability to grasp something, another to let go of something and the third defied you to teach them. The willing were able to accelerate their learning by suspending judgement, letting go of the outcomes and making up their minds without bias on the emerging information.

> GET THIS:
> IF YOU WANT TO LEARN MORE LEAVE
> YOUR EGO OUTSIDE THE DOOR

73 *The Sceptical Agnostic*

The sceptical agnostic, being given a quick preview of the next life by Doubting Thomas, was brought to a mansion in which there were two large rooms.

In one room people were sitting around, lean and mean, crying and wailing, moaning and groaning, whinging and cribbing about how unfair the afterlife was. There was plenty of food but the long spoons they had would not reach their mouths. They bemoaned the dreadful standard of engineering, the poor manufacturing capability, the lack of customer awareness, the absence of any quality control and the total inability of management to get good staff.

In the adjoining room people were good humoured, happy, content, chatting to one another and had a very positive outlook. They were sitting around with long spoons but were well fed.

'What's this?' the agnostic asked.

'Well, you may not believe it,' answered Thomas with a wry smile. 'This is Heaven. Everything in here is the same except here they feed one another.'

SO YOU THINK YOU'VE GOT IT ...

Jean Vanier, a Jesuit noted for both his great work for people with severe disabilities, and his organisational prowess, says, 'It is extremely difficult to bring about organisational transformation without first building

73 *The Sceptical Agnostic*

community.' Collaboration is difficult for it involves everybody giving up something in pursuit of a common purpose. What becomes clear after a while is that there is a tension between individual autonomy and group commitment. What needs to be established is the balance between meeting the needs of the individual and meeting the needs of the group or organisation.

> GET THIS:
> COOPERATING CAN BE HEAVEN AND
> TERRITORIALISM CAN BE HELL

74 Freddy Flies to Florida

Freddy the frog was bright. I mean 'bright' bright, intelligent, and proud of it. He was good looking and meticulous about his dress, wore designer suits and had his voice trained; a little hint of Dublin 4 in his croak. He was tired of Irish winters, the short days and the cold, and was envious of the wild Irish geese who headed off to sunny Florida every winter. 'Florida, Florida, what I would give to go to Florida,' thought Freddy.

Freddy had a flash, another flash, of brilliance. He asked his two friends, the geese, to fly him to Florida, no frills, just get him to Florida. He tied the ends of a long cord to a leg of Goosey and Gandi, stuck a bit of sham-rock onto their tails for good luck, put the centre of the cord in his mouth, gave the thumbs up and off they flew.

All was going well but it was tough, boy was it tough, leaving behind the west coast of Ireland, the green island, all the things he loved: the wet, the damp, the pools by the roadside, the green fields, the shallow ditches, his family, his friends and his boozing buddies.

All was going well until they hit the east coast of America and someone on the ground noticed the strange but wondrous sight overhead. 'Look at that!' shouted the dumbstruck woman to her friends. 'That's unbelievable, fantastic, amazing. Whose idea was that?'

Freddy, to show how clever he was, opened his mouth and shouted, 'Me-e-e-e-e-e-e-e!' dropped the cord from his mouth and fell to the ground with a thud.

SO YOU THINK YOU'VE GOT IT ...

What stops things happening in organisations is territorialism, competition and a concern over what proportion of the credit the various players will get if the project is successful. This often takes place long before anything has been achieved.

GET THIS:

ALMOST ANYTHING CAN BE ACHIEVED IF YOU DON'T MIND WHO GETS THE CREDIT

75 Ronnie the Rabbit

Ronnie, the rabbit, lived on the golf course in Bettys-town, County Meath. He was in his formative years and was quite inexperienced. Life was unexciting there, except for the odd wayward golfball swishing past. Generally speaking, Ronnie felt it safer but even more boring to be on the fairways.

The only bit of real excitement was the passing of the Dublin–Belfast Enterprise Express sixteen times a day. His mother had warned him of the dangers of going too close to the tracks. One day while out on his own he ventured between the lines and stared head on at the oncoming Express. As it came closer to him it seemed to suddenly speed up and caught Ronnie by surprise. Startled, he jumped out of the way but just as the train vanished in an instant, so did his tail.

Ashamed and disappointed that he hadn't paid more attention to his mother, he went back to recover his tail. Getting more and more distracted, he was overjoyed to finally glimpse his tail on the far side of the tracks. He bounded across the tracks, picked up his tail and in a flash the Enterprise Express coming in the opposite direction whisked past, taking his head with it.

SO YOU THINK YOU'VE GOT IT ...

A bad experience is tough enough but to go back to the scene of the crime and have it re-enacted is unforgiv-

75 Ronnie the Rabbit

able. Listen to those who have your interest at heart; sometimes your mother knows best. Organisations are full of ghosts walking around, carrying their heads under their arms, with nobody giving them sympathy or paying a bit of attention to them, largely because they brought the trouble on themselves.

GET THIS:
A KICK ON THE BEHIND IS HARD TO TAKE
BUT DON'T LET IT DO YOUR HEAD IN

Chapter 10
The Blindingly Obvious

Malachy, salesman of the year, noted for the hand-kerchief in his breast pocket, his keen observation skills and his ability to quickly close a sale, was given the unenviable task of tutoring a rookie trainee in door-to-door selling techniques in Dublin's Foxrock area. 'The product doesn't really matter,' he said. 'The key thing is to engage the person with disposable income into the sales conversation as quickly as possible. Turn a need into a want, close the sale and get a sizable deposit up front.'

Malachy had sold items as varied as plots of land in South Africa and broadband in Brooklyn to the unsuspecting public, so selling power hoses to clean cobblelock driveways at a fifty per cent discount seemed a relatively easy number in upmarket Foxrock.

He emphasised to Norman, his protégé, the importance of getting into the potential buyer's mind. There were such things as benefits and features and you could use these to your advantage if you knew what your customer's likes, dislikes and interests were. Information was the key. Keep the client talking and answer a question with a question where possible. It could be power hoses today and fridges tomorrow but it was all about high-pressure sales at the end of the day. Having completed his pep talk, he suggested to Norman that he would take the first call while Norman should keenly observe the transaction.

Malachy walked up the avenue to the front door,

with Norman a respectful pace behind. He pressed the doorbell and to his amazement the door was opened by a fourteen year old boy dressed in a silk lounging gown with a half-filled brandy glass in one hand and a lit Cuban cigar in the other. 'Yes, what can I do for you?' asked the boy.

Catching his breath and composing himself, Malachy calmly enquired, 'Is your father in?'

The boy paused for a moment and in total disbelief replied, 'What do you think?'

SO YOU THINK YOU'VE GOT IT ...

Selling is tricky, expect the unexpected and adjust your approach. Techniques are all very well but are of little value when you come up against the unexpected and are thrown back on your own resources. The sales process is dozens of 'no's with the occasional 'yes' thrown in here and there. That's why children never accept 'no' for an answer, they know there is a 'yes' in there somewhere if you are determined enough to find it. Subtlety, the art of getting the information you need without being offensive, is a great help in getting to 'yes'!

GET THIS:
GETTING TO YES IS EASY, IF YOU WORK REALLY HARD AT IT

Busy place, Heaven on a Friday. There are two queues waiting to gain entrance through the gates, one long and one very short. The long one is the hen-pecked husbands' queue and the shorter one, traditionally, is the assertive husbands' queue. The gatekeeper, the dependable Archangel Gabriel, spent several hours interviewing the hen-pecked queue as, in his experience, they tended to give the most convenient and predictable answers. For a break, Gabriel decided to go to the shorter queue. To his surprise a man had been standing there all alone for some hours. He asked the shy, tired and timid looking man, 'What are you doing here?'

'I really don't know, my wife told me to stand in this queue, so you better ask her,' he hesitatingly replied.

SO YOU THINK YOU'VE GOT IT ...

It is important to know who is speaking for whom. If somebody is taking a stand they are often standing alone so there is generally a good reason for it but it is not always obvious. A primary consideration in interpreting communication is the credibility of the source. Make sure it is the ventriloquist you are paying attention to and not the dummy. Independence of mind is usually a great asset in communicating clearly but not everyone has that luxury.

GET THIS:
BE SLOW TO ACCEPT THINGS AT FACE VALUE

Johannsen was living on the border between Finland and Russia at the end of the Second World War. When the border was being redrawn, Russian troops arrived at his door and the colonel in charge said threateningly, 'We can draw the border line around the front of the house and your home will be in Russia, or to the back of the house and your home will be in Finland. Which do you want?'

The wily old Johannsen humbly instructed, 'Draw it to the back of the house, for an old man like me could never survive another Russian winter.'

SO YOU THINK YOU'VE GOT IT ...

Survival is an instinctive process but sometimes you have to give it a helping hand. You will be surprised when your back is to the wall and you keep your courage, how creative you become. When the odds are stacked against you, diplomacy and creativity are a better option than confrontation.

GET THIS:
THE INSTINCT OF LIFE IS SURVIVAL

After the weekly audit was completed in Heaven, Michael, the archangel, went down to Hell and enquired of Lucifer, 'Have you got a Pat Murphy here?'

'I have,' replied Lucifer.

'From Sallynoggin, Dublin, Ireland?' asked Michael.

'Yes,' replied Lucifer.

'In that case,' said Michael apologetically, 'We have made a terrible mistake. We sent you down the wrong Pat Murphy and we would like to get him back.'

'Get lost,' said Lucifer. 'He is the best man we have; diligent, resourceful, punctual, an organiser, a leader, a high energy person with a great attitude, a big future and he is not leaving here.'

Michael, taken somewhat aback by Lucifer's confrontational and uncooperative behaviour, got on his high horse, 'If that's the way you want it, we will take it to the ombudsman but I'm warning you, JC won't appreciate your unreasonable attitude. He will pull out all the stops, spare no expense, will employ the very best lawyers and roast you,' said Michael with some relish.

Lucifer laughed and exclaimed, 'Would you ever have a tither of wit, Michael, where will JC get a good lawyer?'

SO YOU THINK YOU'VE GOT IT ...

Good staff are very hard to get and sometimes we are fortunate enough to come across them by accident. If

79 *Lucifer*

they are outstanding, the head-hunter is not very far away. The predator will use charm and seduction first. If that does not work he may well resort to strong-arm tactics. If you are confronted by threatening behaviour, assess the intent and capability of the protagonist because you should go to no end of trouble to keep the right people. If you haven't got them you should go to no end of trouble to get them. Ask Lucifer, he is the head-hunter *par excellence*.

> GET THIS:
> IT IS WORTH FIGHTING TO HOLD ON TO
> GOOD STAFF

As a former athlete and a racehorse owner, I learned early in life the value of the health and care of feet, both for man and horse. The locals in my area had an expression: no foot, no horse. In my twenties, I began to experience major problems with my own feet: irritable skin, blisters, corns, sore heels and pains in my insteps. This was all exacerbated by tendon trouble. I used an assortment of remedies including creams, ointments and insoles recommended by specialists in the conventional and alternative medical fields in both Ireland and the USA – all without success. Lo and behold, all the oils, ointments and creams began to work when I changed my shoe size to take account of the growth of my feet from size nine to size nine and a half broad fitting.

SO YOU THINK YOU'VE GOT IT ...

When addressing problems, a lot of time is spent concentrating on the wrong solutions because the presenting symptoms are accepted as the real problem. People are said to be a company's most valuable asset, but rarely are they treated as such. They are often seen as the problem but rarely as part of the solution. Most human problems have humane solutions, not system ones. It takes a sensitive organisation with its eyes focused on more than shareholder value to recognise this and act accordingly.

GET THIS:
ADDRESS THE PROBLEM NOT THE SYMPTOM

It was late spring and Tom Brown, a farmer from west Clare, was about to celebrate his birthday. A bachelor, an environmentalist, good fun and a gentle soul by nature, Tom was much loved by his friends and neighbours. His kind nature somehow gave him a way with animals and his reputation had spread far beyond the county boundaries.

This was a special birthday, Tom's sixtieth, and the farmyard animals could not contain their excitement and fervently wished to add their bit to the festivities. The works committee, made up of a representative of every working animal on the farm, called a meeting in advance of the big occasion. Everybody had their say. The cock suggested he would not crow that day, a major sacrifice. The sheep suggested they would huddle together, count one another and make their own way down to the farmyard. The cows said they would make the supreme effort to give Tom a lie-in – something he had never experienced – and sacrifice being milked that morning. The dog suggested that if everyone behaved, he would go down to the village early and collect the morning paper.

'Good idea,' enthused Porkie the lazy pig trying to bring some closure to the meeting, fearing where it might be heading.

'It's not good, it's bloody brilliant,' added Henrietta the enthusiastic chicken, known to her friends as Hen. 'A lie-in, a read of the morning papers, followed by a sizzling Irish cooked breakfast of bacon, egg and sausage in bed. What more could a man ask for!' she cackled and immediately began to organise the committee.

'Hold your horses!' shouted the disgruntled Porkie, fearing the meeting might run away with the idea. 'This is not fair,' he exclaimed, looking Hen directly in the eye, 'You and your bloody free range eggs, you're only making a contribution, mine would be a total commitment.'

SO YOU THINK YOU'VE GOT IT ...

Some people are, of their very nature, committed and others are highly participative. Those who are committed tend to be very single-minded about a limited number of causes, and they need to be careful to ensure the cause does not burn them up. It's called 'burn out'. Those who actively participate can participate widely because what they contribute to the cause usually comes from the world of ideas and their energy can be replenished following a good night's sleep. High participation has a tendency to lead to very demanding commitments being made, usually on behalf of others, not through any sense of mischievousness but because those participating are enthusiastic in their support of good ideas.

GET THIS:
IT IS EASY TO COMMIT ON OTHER PEOPLE'S BEHALF

José and Manuel, Spanish tourists in a pub in Connemara, were marvelling at the beauty of the Irish language. José asked a native speaker if there was an equivalent in the Gaelic tongue for the Spanish word 'mañana'. The native speaker, somewhat confused, asked José to explain the meaning of the word 'mañana' in English to him.

'Well,' said José, 'it is quite difficult but it sort of means "tomorrow or the next day or the following day", it means "whenever", it means "in God's own time".'

The Gaelic speaker reflected on this for a while, his eyes suddenly lit up and he said, 'Do you know, I don't believe there is any word in the Gaelic language that conveys quite that same sense of urgency!'

SO YOU THINK YOU'VE GOT IT ...

People's attitude to time can be biblical, precise or just plain sloppy. People say they will get back to you in five minutes, will talk to you tomorrow, or will make a decision by the end of the week. Deadlines are simply guidelines for some and carved in stone for others. You have to check the milestones or they quickly become millstones. Ninety per cent of success is said to be 'just turning up' and that means committing to your deadlines, not mañana.

GET THIS:
BE LIKE ROBINSON CRUSOE AND HAVE YOUR WORK DONE BY FRIDAY

Young Paddy tentatively went to his second confession in Rolestown in North County Dublin with his godmother, Auntie Nora. While cycling home a rat ran straight across the front wheel of his bike. Startled he shouted, 'Jesus, a rat!' His Auntie Nora, horrified at his taking the holy name in vain and his tendency towards bad language, marched him straight back to confession to the parish priest.

Embarrassed, scared and fearful at having returned so soon, Paddy mumbled his grave offence to the surprised priest, 'I took the name of the Lord, our God in vain.'

'What did you say?' boomed the priest impatiently.

Paddy guiltily confessed a second time.

'I still can't hear you, I can't hear you, speak up boy,' exclaimed the now irritated priest.

Plucking up courage the boy shouted, 'Jesus, a rat.'

'Christ, where?' roared the priest as he exited the confession box in total panic.

SO YOU THINK YOU'VE GOT IT ...

We are often asked to present ourselves to authority when we are a bag of nerves and when fear and impatience are the dominant emotions. When we are nervous or fearful, things get out of proportion and dialogue often becomes minimal or impossible. Sometimes we have to slow down, get hold of the situation, organise things and create a safe environment where we get proper attention and are listened to. Shouting on anybody's behalf doesn't really help, it only adds to the panic.

> **GET THIS:**
> EVERYBODY HAS BUTTERFLIES; THE TRICK
> IS TO GET THEM FLYING IN FORMATION

84 *Scarlet the Scorpion*

Scarlet, the scorpion, wanders over to the bank of the lake and asks the frog if he will take her over to the far side. The frog recoils in absolute horror. 'Are you mad or what?' he exclaims. 'I will be halfway over and you will sting me and poison me!'

'No,' said the charming Scarlet, 'I won't do that, it doesn't make sense. If I did that not only would you die but I would drown.'

'I suppose,' thought the frog on reflection. 'Ok, just this once. Hop on my back and let's go.' When they were halfway across the lake, Scarlet stung the frog and as the frog keeled over he cried out in desperation to the scorpion, 'Oh why, oh why did you do that?'

'I couldn't help it, I just couldn't resist it, it's my nature,' splurted the drowning Scarlet.

SO YOU THINK YOU'VE GOT IT ...

Nature does exactly what it says on the tin. While logic is a very powerful argument it doesn't always hold up. When well intentioned, it is easier to make the intellectual commitment than the emotional one. But if the emotional commitment is not made you haven't got agreement, what you've got is the beginnings of betrayal.

GET THIS:
THE BEST PREDICTOR OF FUTURE BEHAVIOUR IS PAST BEHAVIOUR

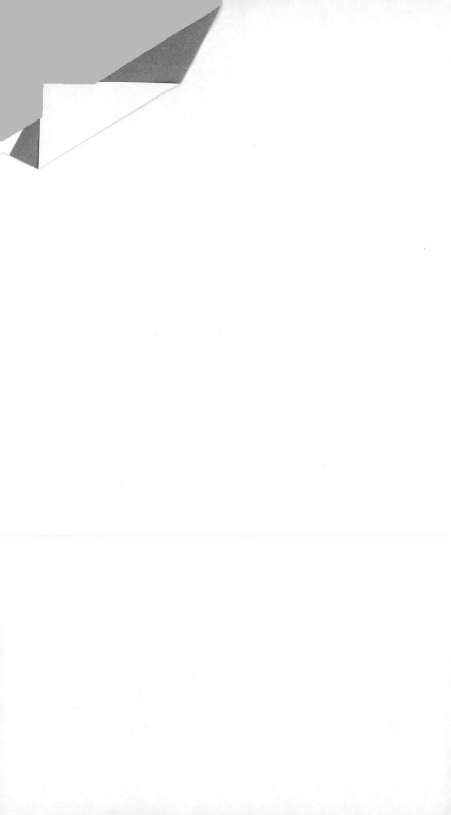

Chapter

Howling at the Mooon

It was a beautiful summer Sunday in May and Michael and Mary went for a walk along the banks of the Dodder. Suddenly they heard the screaming of a baby in the river. They ran to the edge and could see this poor little mite in a pink babygro flaying about in complete panic. Michael took immediate action and got Mary to wade in. She grabbed the baby and handed it to Michael. He took Mary's outstretched hand and helped her onto dry land. Mary quickly took the baby from him and gave it the kiss of life. She then laid it down tenderly and began to dry herself off.

Suddenly there was another scream, another baby, another rescue operation called for. Michael organised Mary once again. Into the river she wades, grabs the baby, makes her way towards Michael, gives him the baby, grasps his outstretched hand and pulls herself exhaustedly to the bank. Yet again Mary takes the baby from Michael, gives it the kiss of life and places it gently beside the first baby. She bursts out crying, tears of joy, tears of tension and, emotionally emptied, finally lies down herself.

Another searing scream is heard, another baby in the river. Michael and Mary are becoming practised now. Michael helps Mary to the water's edge, she rescues the baby, lets Michael give it the kiss of life and meanwhile tries to gather her wits and regain some composure.

Forty screaming babies later, forty rescues later and Mary has had more than enough. On the forty-first scream, totally exhausted and in anger, she calls up her very last ounce of energy and yells, 'Michael, will you ever head off upstream and see who is throwing those babies into the river!'

SO YOU THINK YOU'VE GOT IT ...

Deal with the downstream problems as a matter of urgency, but deal with the upstream causes as a matter of priority. Handling crises can become a career, however it is never ending and ultimately totally exhausting. Panic sets in, scapegoating takes place and those in the front line, regardless of the energy or effort they put in, get blamed. Support the front line people. Meanwhile, move upstream to cut off the cause of the problem at its source.

GET THIS:
MOST DOWNSTREAM PROBLEMS HAVE
UPSTREAM SOLUTIONS

Two people in dispute appeared before Solomon in the belief he would shed some light on their case. After the first person had presented his side of the story, Solomon observed to his satisfaction, 'You are right.'

When the second person presented the story from his particular point of view, Solomon declared to his surprise, 'You are right.'

At that, they proclaimed in frustration, 'We cannot both be right!'

Solomon yet again replied, 'You are right.'

SO YOU THINK YOU'VE GOT IT ...

Unconventional thinking or thinking outside the box is rarely given enough space in this analytical world of ours. The most desirable attributes for people living in a complex world are tolerance of ambiguity and the ability to synergise information and make connections from different fields of knowledge. Einstein stated that in his opinion, imagination was more important than knowledge. Creative solutions come only when we give ourselves permission to live on the edge and to work at the frontiers of our imagination. Often we have to be jolted towards imaginative thinking and creative solutions.

GET THIS:
CREATIVITY IS A DIVERGENT PROCESS

87 *Horse Sense*

A weary tourist's hired car breaks down in the depths of rural Ireland. Totally mystified, he lifts the bonnet despairingly and peers into the engine. A voice calls out, 'Clean the spark plugs.'

He looks around and there, standing all alone, head over the ditch, ears alert and peering at him, are two horses, one black and one white, and apparently not another person in sight. 'I could have sworn I heard a voice,' he says.

'You did, clean the spark plugs and start the engine,' instructs the voice.

Confused, he does as he's bid and to his utter amazement the engine starts. He slams down the bonnet, jumps into the car and drives off at full speed. He screeches to a halt at the first pub he meets, rushes into the bar, grabs a bar stool and orders a double brandy. The dumbfounded tourist excitedly recounts the story to an unimpressed barman. 'Was it the white horse?' the barman asks nonchalantly.

'I think it was,' said the mystified visitor. 'But what difference does it make?'

'Well,' answered the barman, 'They say that black horse is absolutely useless when it comes to cars!'

Leonardo da Vinci believed context was everything. Content is meaningless without the context. The barman believed the horses could talk so the content then became relevant while the tourist, knowing in his own mind they couldn't, became increasingly impatient with the barman's emphasis on the seemingly irrelevant detail. If people can agree the context, it is then much easier to get understanding on the content. Far too much time is spent negotiating and discussing the content precisely because far too little time is spent on clarifying and agreeing the context. If people see the big picture it's easier for them to imagine where they might or might not fit in. Ask Leonardo, he felt it entirely appropriate to fit himself into 'The Last Supper'!

> GET THIS:
> CONTEXT IS WHAT GIVES MEANING
> TO CONTENT

The artist Tony O'Malley, who died in 2003, tells the story of the trials and tribulations of living in digs in Limerick while working for the bank in his first job: 'One of the things about being a lodger with any fellow lodger, was the difficulty of discussing anything with them. They could argue about everything, but wouldn't discuss anything! You'd be shouted down and everything was potential heresy.'

SO YOU THINK YOU'VE GOT IT ...

To quote George Bernard Shaw, 'He is a great conversationalist, he would listen to you all day.' The art of listening is central to good conversation and good conversation is said to be one of the finer attributes of the Celts. Arguing generally demonstrates the absence of listening and does not contribute to the building of empathy and connection. Ninety per cent of good business is good dialogue. It is about discussing and not arguing; it is not about winning or losing but about building a commonality of purpose. In the final analysis it is about creating an environment in which the business of the day can be constructively discussed.

GET THIS:
ARGUING IS NOT DISCUSSING

Annie, from west Limerick, was all excited. She was on her first ever plane journey, an all expenses paid holiday from Shannon to New York to visit her recently married and successful son in Manhattan; her white haired boy, the apple of her eye.

She was seated next to a well dressed, tall, elegant and obviously sophisticated gentleman, totally engaged with his laptop computer. She gently enquired as a conversation opener, 'Are you from the States?' He answered 'no' without shifting his gaze from the computer, now set up and sitting on the tray directly in front of him.

Sometime later, after studying him intensely, Annie volunteered, 'You can tell me, I have eight children of my own you know and I am a pretty good judge of people. You are from the States, aren't you?'

He sharply declared, 'No, I am not.'

She continued to observe him for several minutes and eventually tapped him gently on the back of his working hand, saying, 'You are definitely from the States, I can tell!'

To get rid of the nuisance and back to the privacy of business on the computer the man frustratingly replied, 'Yes, I am from the States, from the state of Nebraska, flying to Kennedy Airport and taking the shuttle limousine to my office in New Jersey,' and promptly buried himself in the important work on his laptop.

Annie continued to stare at him, this time with some

pride and said, 'You know, that's absolutely amazing. I knew it all along but you certainly don't look it!'

The self-fulfilling prophecy exercises all our minds. We come to our own conclusions and then find some way to arrive at them, even if it requires an unbelievable fleetness of foot to do so. The acting out of the self-fulfilling prophecy is particularly prevalent in Performance Management. Staff either live up to or down to the reality of our expectations of them and we don't always consider fully the part we play in that and the impact it has on performance.

GET THIS:
REALITY IS NOT WHAT IS, BUT WHAT WE HAVE DECIDED IT IS

John called over to his neighbour, Peter, who was chopping wood, 'Peter, may I borrow your axe?'

'No,' replied Peter. 'I need it to shave with.'

Peter's wife overheard the conversation in disbelief and confronted Peter on his return to the house. 'Peter, that was a terrible excuse to give John for not lending him the axe.'

'Well, my dear,' said Peter, 'It's like this: when you don't want to do something, one excuse is as good as another.'

SO YOU THINK YOU'VE GOT IT ...

There is a difference between truth and honesty. In truth John did not want to lend the axe. In all honesty he did not come up with a great excuse to mask the truth. One of the most subtle forms of resistance to change is not outright opposition, but the half truth, and sweet unreasonableness. To break the change momentum, it is in the interest of many to slow things down, to delay, to confuse, to refer, to bring to committee or to tie up in procedural wrangles. A coalition of unlikely partners consciously or unconsciously will often emerge and form an agreed strategy of smoke and mirrors to keep things exactly as they are. Stay alert, if you snooze you lose.

GET THIS:
THERE ARE A THOUSAND WAYS OF SAYING NO AND ONLY ONE WAY OF SAYING YES

91 *The Super Bowl*

The Super Bowl finals bring back memories to me of another story about Joe Montana of the San Francisco 49ers. Joe played quarterback, and was one of the all time great sportsmen in my lifetime, up there with George Best, Lester Piggott, Michael Jordan, Mohammed Ali, Tiger Woods, D.J. Carey and, more recently, Brian O'Driscoll.

Having returned to the dressing room after a particularly gruelling and bruising encounter he threw his helmet in the corner, took off his shoulder pads, dragged his bruised body over to the sink and, looking into the mirror, thought, 'There has to be an easier way of meeting congenial people of my own age group.'

SO YOU THINK YOU'VE GOT IT ...

In this life there are players and spectators. For every thirty players in the stadium there could be thirty, forty or fifty thousand spectators. For every hundred employees in an organisation there is often only one who really wants to make a difference, stand out from the pack and make an impact. Players get hustled, bustled and bruised. There is an easier way: become a spectator, but be warned, it's not as much fun; you never experience an adrenalin rush but it's a safer place to be in the heat of battle.

GET THIS:
IF IT'S THE EASY LIFE YOU ARE AFTER, BE A SPECTATOR

92 Missionary Zeal

There was a drink problem in the West of Ireland and the women in the local community decided to do something about it. They invited Father Mathew from Cork to the village to give a talk on the evils of drink.

The usual suspects were rounded up and Father Mathew started. He denounced drinking, the hardship it brought to communities, families, relationships, and the untold damage it did to the individuals themselves. To drive home the point he placed two large glasses in front of him and filled one with water and the other with poteen. He took a snuffbox from his pocket and took two worms out of the box; he dropped one into the water and the other into the poteen.

The worm in the water swam around happily enjoying himself, while the worm in the poteen immediately shrivelled up and died.

'Well now,' Father Mathew enquired, pounding the table, 'What's the point of all this?' Frightened and intimidated nobody answered. He again pounded the table and boomed 'What is the moral to be taken from this?'

A small, stocky man at the back of the hall rose slowly to his unsteady feet and answered, 'Obviously, Father, if you drink enough poteen you will never suffer from worms?'

92 *Missionary Zeal*

Your world view determines how you interpret events and the resulting actions you take. Captain Tim Foster, trainer of three Aintree Grand National winners, once said, 'I am a pessimist and unfortunately the worst thing about being a pessimist is there's nothing you can do about it'. A huge mind shift is required to disrupt embedded thinking and allow us to visualise other options. Where everybody is thinking the same, nobody is thinking very much. Personal insight comes from deep within our own experience, a flash of brilliance perhaps! It often provides us with a different view of the world which makes perfect sense to us, but not always to others; however it does encourage others to think.

GET THIS:
PERCEPTION IS REALITY

Chapter 12

Ha Ha Ha! or Aha!

93 *The Dub's Your Only Man*

An eccentric Dublin teddy boy, complete with drain-pipe trousers, winkle picker shoes, leather jacket and oiled brushed back crew-cut hair, was recruited for the war in Korea. As he made his way unobtrusively through the countryside, anxious not to disturb the natives or draw unnecessary attention to himself, out from behind a tree popped a Korean, who put a gun to his head and cocked the trigger. The teddy boy didn't panic. In one movement he whipped a flick-knife from his pocket, released the blade and went 'swish' across the Korean's neck.

The Korean pulled back, laughed and said with a grin, 'You've missed!'

'Wait till you shake your fecking head,' retorted the teddy boy.

SO YOU THINK YOU'VE GOT IT ...

It is important to recognise that all managerial positions are temporary. One of the key attributes of successful managers is the ability to get into a department, get the work done and move on before anyone notices. Most managerial work boils down to a series of projects which have a beginning and an end; a certain life span. It is important to know not alone where the project starts but where it finishes. They either get finished or become a career. If the finish line keeps moving, you will collapse eventually and die from frustration or exhaustion.

93 *The Dub's Your Only Man*

Work to a deadline, it avoids endless suffering. Ideally your life span should exceed that of the projects. Finish and move on before someone slits your throat.

> GET THIS:
> TO SUCCEED YOU NEED TO BE
> VERY GOOD AT WHAT YOU DO

Mrs Sutton's son, Willy, was bright and personable. She had high hopes of him becoming a doctor one day. He had a good bedside manner and a sharp analytical mind. But, like many a student, he took to the wayward path in his early teens to such an extent he became a noted bank robber.

When asked why he robbed banks given the risks involved, he replied, 'Because that is where the money is.'

Though Mrs Sutton died disappointed before Willy reached his full potential, she no doubt took some satisfaction from the fact that Willy finally made his mark on the medical profession. In medicine, 'Sutton's Law' is the name given to the principle of going straight to the most likely diagnosis.

Mrs Sutton, an independent woman, knew well there was nothing as emancipating as a little money of your own and her child had learned the lesson well. However, young Willy didn't quite understand the nature of the problem and how to remedy it.

Fixing the problem tends to address the symptoms and often only requires unilateral action, but solving it requires you to define the problem with all its complexities and then take the required action which is frequently collaborative in nature. Willy's failing was not that he confronted the issue of the redistribution of wealth, but that he sought a simple solution to it and, in trying to fix it, he took the law into his own hands.

> GET THIS:
> WHEN SOMETHING IRRATIONAL IS
> CONSISTENTLY GOING ON, THERE IS
> USUALLY A SOLID REASON FOR IT

The taxi driver picked up the casually dressed customer at 7 a.m. in Bray, Co. Wicklow (a town in its own right, but expanding quickly as a satellite of Dublin).

'Heuston Station,' the passenger announced. 'I'm in a hurry. I have to catch the 7.45 train from Dublin to Cork, so be lively and if you get me there in time I'll give you €20 extra.'

'It will be close,' answered the driver, pressing his foot on the accelerator, 'but we could be lucky because that Dublin to Cork train always leaves late,' he added with some optimism.

'I know,' said his passenger, 'I'm the driver!'

SO YOU THINK YOU'VE GOT IT ...

Time keeping is a power statement and it demonstrates respect or lack of respect. Don't assume that your time is more important than the other person's. Those who arrive late either think they cannot be done without or don't really care. In the final analysis it is disrespectful to others and shows a lack of common courtesy. It is best to be on time for you will be noticed for the right reasons, have a better grasp of reality, and you may, in due course, get your just rewards.

GET THIS:
DON'T BE LATE, EVEN IF YOU ARE IN CHARGE

96 *Sick as a Parrot*

Margaret, a proud Mayo woman through and through, was especially proud of her three sons who were deemed by the neighbours and all their friends to be a success in life. The boys, emigrants to the United States, were hard working, always thoughtful and, in more recent times, frequent visitors to Westport, their hometown.

This visit had special significance for it was their widowed mother's ninetieth birthday, a special occasion by any standard and an appropriate time to show their mother the love and high regard they had for her.

Peter, the eldest, flamboyant by nature, decided to mark the occasion by giving his mother a new house, indeed more a mansion, with five bedrooms and five bathrooms. Realising that upkeep might be a problem he also supplied kitchen staff and a butler as part of this gift.

Paul, not to be outdone, gave her a gift of a new top of the range Mercedes Benz with a driver available twenty-four hours a day. Paul, a sensitive type, knowing his mother to be a proud woman, also provided her with ten free driving lessons to prevent her feeling inadequate.

Simon, the youngest, had been thinking about the occasion for some time. His mother was very religious, a devout Catholic, and last thing at night she read an excerpt from her Bible and reflected on it, before drifting off to sleep. Her faculties were in slow but steady decline; most noticeably her deteriorating eyesight which was accelerated by the development of cataracts. He decided to give her a parrot.

96 *Sick as a Parrot*

Now Polly the Parrot was no ordinary parrot, for she, like Simon, was a graduate of Glenstal Abbey, trained in Catechetics and fully conversant with both Old and New Testament. Polly had a memory bank superior to most computers and her diction and intonation were exceptional. She was currently mastering the art of Gregorian chant. It took all of Simon's charm to separate Glenstal from their precious Polly, but given the uniqueness of the occasion, the thoughtfulness of Simon and his past generosity to the Abbey, they made the ultimate sacrifice and agreed to give Simon the parrot with their blessing.

'Polly, Genesis 2:16?' Simon would prompt.

Polly would start, 'Then the Lord God said, it is not good that man should be alone.'

'Truly amazing!' thought Simon. 'Polly, John 14:18?'

'I will not leave you desolate I will come to you ...'

Unbelievable. Simon marvelled at the pleasure he knew his mother would get from Polly, not alone as a substitute for her failing hearing, eyesight and memory, but also for the company Polly would provide in her final years. It was the perfect gift.

After the birthday celebrations Margaret, as she was accustomed to doing, wrote briefly as follows to her three boys on their return to the United States.

To Peter: 'Thank you for the wonderful gift of the house and the servants for my birthday. As you know I was born in this, our family home, and humble and all as it is I hope to die in it as your dear father did. I have let the help go but I truly appreciate your generosity. Mother.'

To Paul: 'There really was no need for you to go to the bother of getting me a car and such an expensive one. As you know I am only fit now to leave the house to attend mass. Paddy our next-door neighbour has been bringing me for thirty years and I look forward to the bit of company on a Sunday. Nevertheless it was most thoughtful of you. Mother.'

To Simon: 'As usual, you got it just right, the chicken was absolutely delicious. Your loving mother.'

SO YOU THINK YOU'VE GOT IT ...

Needs and wants are different. You may think you know what other people's needs are and how to meet them and indeed you may. Their wants are another matter entirely. Where there is resistance, it can take a lot of energy and effort to turn a need into a want and there are times you may not succeed. If you are repeating yourself and beginning to sound like a parrot give up, compromise, meet the want first and see can you agree on and satisfy some part of the need later. Good is often good enough and is less exhausting than striving endlessly for unattainable perfection. Settle for a chicken.

GET THIS:
PERFECTIONISM IS THE ENEMY OF GOOD

97 *The Wheelbarrow*

Joe left the building site once or twice a day pushing a wheelbarrow. Suspicious that something was amiss, Security searched the wheelbarrow daily for spades, shovels, pickaxes, bricks or anything that might usefully be taken from a building site, but found nothing to be concerned about. Stocktaking at the end of the year, however, revealed a shortage of 300 wheelbarrows!

SO YOU THINK YOU'VE GOT IT ...

In organisational life, both the detail and the big picture are important. You can see it all, yet miss the essence because you cannot piece the bits together. In pursuit of continuous improvement, there are two questions we should have uppermost in our minds: 'Do we know what we are looking for?' and 'Would we recognise it when we saw it?'

GET THIS:
SEEING IS NOT RECOGNISING

98 *With God's Help*

S ammy, a hard working, diligent man, had been saving all his life to buy a farm of his own and to be independent. He was fortunate to be able to afford a derelict farm in his native County Monaghan. After two years hard work he invited his local minister to inspect the premises.

As they drove in the front gate, Sammy explained that the driveway, previously a mud path, and hardly accessible by foot, was freshly gravelled with new railings on either side. 'That's a lovely job,' said the minister, 'and I can see God's hand in all of this.'

On entering the hay barn, Sammy pointed out the new concrete floor and the repaired panels on the roof. 'That's a fine job Sammy, I can see God's work in all of this,' commented the minister.

Sammy brought the minister to the nearly fifteen-acre pasture, newly drained, adjoining ditch removed and fresh grass sown the previous autumn. 'Well,' asked Sammy, standing back rather proudly, 'What do you think?'

The minister reflected for a moment and said 'Sammy, you've done well, sure God was with you.'

Irritated and feeling put down, Sammy quickly retorted, 'Well minister, with all due respect, you should have seen this place when God had it to himself!'

98 *With God's Help*

Gary Player, having won three consecutive US tournaments with more than his fair share of luck, is famously quoted as saying, 'I've noticed that the more I practise the luckier I get.' Luck has been described as 'the place where preparation meets opportunity'. Successful people frequently credit their success to a mixture of preparation and perspiration, which other people describe as luck. Wasn't God lucky Sammy bought the farm?

GET THIS:
SUCCESS DEMANDS PREPARATION,
PERSPIRATION AND LUCK

99 The Last Laugh

Johnny, a countryman, was being interviewed for a big job in Dublin. No representations had been made on his behalf, but a quiet word, nevertheless, was put in for him in the right place.

The interviewer said, 'John I will ask you one question and if you answer it correctly I will give you the job.' The interviewer tried to assist him as best he could, framing a country friendly question: 'Johnny, if I gave you a pair of ducks and later gave you two more, how many ducks would you have in all?'

Johnny thought for a moment and quietly answered, 'Five.'

The interviewer frowned, rubbed his brow and explained, 'Two plus two makes four, have you got that?'

'Yes,' said Johnny assuredly.

'Ok, I will try again. If I gave you a pair of ducks and later on gave you two more, how many ducks would you have?'

Johnny reflected even longer and eventually answered, 'Five.'

'Good God,' said the frustrated interviewer, 'Didn't I tell you that two plus two equals four?'

'Yes,' said Johnny, 'But that's not what you asked me. You asked me how many ducks would I have? I have one duck at home plus the four ducks you gave me, that, by my reckoning, is five.'

99 *The Last Laugh*

SO YOU THINK YOU'VE GOT IT ...

Patronising people normally stems from arrogance or being out of touch. Get out from behind the desk, it is a bad place from which to view the world; you will never have the full picture, only the statistics. Truth is rarely found in statistics and, at the end of the day, you may find yourself missing a few ducks.

> GET THIS:
> PATRONISING PEOPLE GENERALLY
> BACKFIRES

Stop Howling at the Moon 199

SO YOU THINK YOU'VE GOT IT ...

GET THIS:

101 The Last Word

Paddy, a devout Catholic, and a large landowner with a bad cough, suddenly fell seriously ill. His young wife, Tricia, with an eye to the future, called the priest urgently and the doctor sometime later. The priest, a fastidious man, gave Paddy the last rites, heard his confession and began to pray into his ear: 'Do you renounce Satan and all his works and pomps?'

Paddy pulled frantically at the priest's sleeve and, with growing irritation yet firm assurance in his faltering voice proclaimed, 'Father, this is no time for somebody in my condition to be antagonising anyone.'

SO YOU THINK YOU'VE GOT IT ...

Your future may be made or unmade in the friends you choose and when you choose them. You are sometimes better off focusing on the job in hand rather than hitching your wagon to a shooting star. It's bad enough falling out with others but foolish to fall out with them on somebody else's behalf. Make as few enemies as you can when your career is in the ascendancy, for you will need all the goodwill you can muster if things take a turn for the worse. Be happy with the choices you make for nothing is as simple as it seems and remember, you have to live with the consequences.

GET THIS:
WORK VERY HARD AT BEING CIRCUMSPECT

Stop Howling at the Moon 201

Final Thought

The early bird catches the worm.
The second mouse gets the cheese.

(Old Irish Saying)

If you have a story to tell and
would be happy to have it included in
the next volume of

Stop Howling at the Moon

please email it, with your name and address, to:

stophowling@onstream.ie

For seminars, keynote speeches, workshops
and consulting services by

Eamon O'Donnell

please contact:

RMS Consulting
11 Sharavogue
Upper Glenageary Road
Glenageary
Co. Dublin
Ireland

or email:

rmsconsulting@eircom.net